T0356132

Praise for *Hacking Advertising*

"Jon Sneider's *Hacking Advertising: How We Learned to Make Ads Without the Agency (And You Can Too)* is a manifesto that redefines what's possible in advertising. As a proven innovator and disruptor, Jon demonstrates how the traditional agency model—often seen as essential—can be streamlined or bypassed entirely, even for the biggest companies in the world. Drawing from his experience leading campaigns at industry giants like Microsoft, Jon exposes inefficiencies, shatters myths, and offers practical tools to create high-impact advertising with less time, fewer resources, and far more control. This book is a must-read for marketing leaders seeking a more streamlined, audience-driven approach to creating impactful marketing assets. It's also a valuable resource for marketing students eager to glimpse the inner workings of Fortune 500 marketing departments. Jon's bare-knuckled storytelling and real-life learning reveal not only how world-class campaigns come to life but also the hidden pitfalls to creativity and alignment within corporate structures. It's a crash course in navigating, innovating, and thriving in modern advertising."

—John Dougherty, Chief Marketing Officer, Brighton Jones Wealth Management

"You can spend the next 20 years going through the school of hard knocks that is marketing leadership, or just cut to the chase and buy Jon Sneider's exceptional book. Part practical playbook, part professional autobiography, *Hacking Advertising* won't just save your organization money—it will save something infinitely more valuable—time!"

—**Richard Stern,** CEO, TuneIn

"Jon Sneider has been improving the way advertising is made for decades, always leveraging the latest technology innovations. This book is great advice for all of us who want advertising to stay ahead of the next wave of innovation."

—**David W. Kenny,** Executive Chairman, Nielsen

"*Hacking Advertising: How We Learned to Make Ads Without the Agency (and You Can Too)* is a groundbreaking guide that challenges the traditional advertising model. Jon Sneider argues that the conventional agency approach is often inefficient and expensive, and he provides a compelling case for brands to take control of their creative production. The book is a treasure trove of practical advice, advocating for the development of internal creative capabilities or partnerships with lean, agile creative production companies.

Sneider emphasizes the importance of quick, iterative processes and the value of frequent market tests to refine and optimize advertising strategies. This book is a must-read for anyone looking to revolutionize their marketing approach and achieve better results through efficiency and effectiveness."

—**Aaron Strout,** Chief Marketing Officer, Real Chemistry

"*Hacking Advertising* takes a closer look at the advertising process, celebrating its successes while addressing areas for improvement. Jon Sneider shares practical solutions for enhancing efficiency and creativity within existing frameworks. It's a thought-provoking read for anyone in marketing or agency leadership."

—**Rob Reilly,** Global Chief Creative Officer, WPP

"Move over Tim Ferriss: Jon Sneider has created the ultimate hack to the bloated traditional agency model and takes us behind the scenes of his career, creating a compelling business case for a more nimble and resourceful approach to developing creative advertising that drives results."

—**Marc Oshima,** Chief Marketing Officer and Co-Founder, AeroFarms

"Advertising is in such flux these days it's hard to describe what an agency is anymore. In *Hacking Advertising*, Jon Sneider details how marketers can save millions with a straight-to-production approach, and how agencies and production companies can adapt to this new world. Creative production shops have smaller teams that move much faster than traditional agencies. They replace focus groups with in-market testing, and swap agency bureaucracy for "GSD" people— seasoned pros who just "Get Shit Done." What's not to like?"

—**Luke Sullivan,** author, *Hey Whipple, Squeeze This: The Classic Guide to Creating Great Advertising*

"Jon Sneider's *Hacking Advertising* is a bold and refreshing take on an industry bogged down by inefficiencies and outdated processes. With his firsthand experiences leading campaigns for global giants like Microsoft, Sneider lays bare the challenges of traditional advertising and offers a clear, actionable blueprint for a better way forward. His hybrid approach to ad production—combining creative and production under one roof—feels not just innovative but essential in today's fast-paced marketing landscape. What sets this book apart is Sneider's ability to make complex topics relatable and engaging. From tales of creating fake snow in Pasadena to navigating the bureaucratic maze of agency politics, his storytelling keeps readers hooked while delivering valuable lessons. The book is packed with practical advice, like eliminating unnecessary middlemen, embracing in-market testing, and rethinking agency relationships, making it a must-read for anyone in marketing or advertising. More than just a guide, *Hacking Advertising* is a call to arms for marketers to reclaim control of their creative processes. It's a book that will leave you inspired, empowered, and ready to create ads that don't just look good but actually make an impact."

—**Scott Erikson,** CEO Manufaktur Marketing, and CMO, Picnic

"You don't need to be in the advertising industry to enjoy and get a ton of value from Jon Sneider's *Hacking Advertising; How We Learned To Make Ads Without the Agency (and You Can Too)*. It's a great book for *everyone*—from college students and incoming interns to seasoned industry professionals—interested in selling, marketing, or advertising *anything*. For the uninitiated industry hopefuls—let this book be your guide to help you navigate your career and speak up for efficiency where it's desperately needed. If you're in the industry and find yourself aggressively nodding while you read, you'll feel affirmed in your frustrations, validated in your desire to do things differently, and equipped with a roadmap to help you build a framework that empowers you and your team to do what you do best."

—**Sydney Williams,** author of *Hiking Your Feelings*, founder of Hiking My Feelings

"This book is for every marketer who's ever asked, 'Why is this so hard?' In *Hacking Advertising*, Jon Sneider dismantles the outdated agency model and replaces it with something better. His insights are sharp, his advice actionable, and his solutions revolutionary."

—Phil Greenwood, CEO Redmond Technology Partners

"As a small business owner trying to scale my services, I found *Hacking Advertising* by Jon Sneider to be an insightful and practical guide. The book demystifies traditional advertising models, offering efficient strategies for creating impactful campaigns without large agencies. Sneider's focus on breaking down silos and integrating creative and production processes is particularly valuable for businesses aiming to grow while maximizing their budgets. His relatable anecdotes and actionable advice make this an empowering read for anyone looking to simplify and elevate their advertising efforts."

—Carl Nelson, CEO and Founder, Visual

"Part memoir, part industry critique, *Hacking Advertising* is the rare book that combines storytelling with strategy. Jon Sneider takes readers through the highs and lows of his career, offering hard-won lessons on how to navigate the complexities of modern advertising. His writing is engaging and relatable, making even the most technical aspects feel approachable. What sets this book apart is its practicality—every chapter offers tools and tips that can be applied immediately. Sneider doesn't just point out what's broken; he shows you how to fix it. This is essential reading for anyone looking to level up their marketing game."

—Greg Olson, Head of Data & Analytics, Clear Channel Outdoor

"Jon Sneider's *Hacking Advertising* is both a powerful critique of the ad industry and a call to action. His experience shines through as he shares insights that will help marketers create better work without the usual headaches."

—Jason Szep, Bureau Chief, Reuters

"Jon presents a no-nonsense, commonsense vision of an agency model that works the way many clients have wished for. An arrangement where the clients' thoughts, expertise, and ideas are as just as welcome and respected as the agency's."

—Rob Rizzo, Creative Strategic Consultant, Marketing Suite Spot

"Jon Sneider's *Hacking Advertising* provides a roadmap for both clients and agencies to adopt a more efficient, cost-effective, and creative-focused approach to advertising production. Jon's experience and insight shows how businesses can produce better creative work faster and with fewer resources, ultimately driving greater success in the market."

—Adam Anderson, Senior Vice President, Growth Marketing, Zscaler

"*Hacking Advertising* is more than a book—it's a game plan for overhauling the status quo. Jon's candor, irreverence, and genuine passion for the craft shine through on every page. If you're tired of bloated processes and big agencies charging huge fees, this book will change your perspective for good. As someone intimately familiar with typical processes (focus groups, big strategy decks, endless approvals) Jon offers a new approach to making advertising that's more agile, affordable, and more performant—non-negotiables in the emerging world of AI creative. If you're fed up with marketing-as-usual, this is your escape plan."

—Paul Campbell, CEO/Founder, Technology Companies

"With experience spanning corporate marketing, agency, and his own creative production company, Jon Sneider brings a rare and invaluable perspective to the chaos of modern advertising. Anyone who's spent even five minutes in the industry knows it's deeply flawed—and only getting worse. Sneider's hands-on insights and pragmatic, no-nonsense approach offer marketers a smarter way to navigate the inefficiencies, frustrations, and dysfunction that plague today's advertising production and agency models."

—J. B. Raftus, Founder and CEO, Outpost Collaborative

"Jon Sneider's *Hacking Advertising* is a masterclass in challenging the status quo. With decades of experience, he expertly identifies the inefficiencies in the traditional advertising model and offers practical solutions for creating world-class campaigns. This book is as much a wake-up call as it is a guidebook for marketers who want to rethink the way they work. Sneider's insights are sharp, his tone refreshingly honest, and his advice actionable. Whether you're a seasoned professional or a newcomer to the industry, this book will inspire you to embrace creativity and efficiency. It's a must-read for anyone who cares about great advertising."

—**Tami Reller,** technology and healthcare
executive and board director

Hacking
Advertising

JON SNEIDER

Hacking Advertising

How We Learned to Make Ads
Without the Agency (and You Can Too)

AN INC.
ORIGINAL

An Inc. Original
New York, New York
www.anincoriginal.com

This work is being published under the An Inc. Original imprint by an exclusive arrangement with Inc. Magazine. Inc. Magazine and the Inc. logo are registered trademarks of Mansueto Ventures, LLC. The An Inc. Original logo is a wholly owned trademark of Mansueto Ventures, LLC.

Distributed by Greenleaf Book Group

For ordering information or special discounts for bulk purchases, please contact Greenleaf Book Group at PO Box 91869, Austin, TX 78709, 512.891.6100.

Design and composition by Greenleaf Book Group
Cover design by Greenleaf Book Group

Publisher's Cataloging-in-Publication data is available.

Print ISBN: 978-1-63909-054-9

eBook ISBN: 978-1-63909-055-6

To offset the number of trees consumed in the printing of our books, Greenleaf donates a portion of the proceeds from each printing to the Arbor Day Foundation. Greenleaf Book Group has replaced over 50,000 trees since 2007.

Printed in the United States of America on acid-free paper

25 26 27 28 29 30 31 32   10 9 8 7 6 5 4 3 2 1

First Edition

This book is dedicated to my wife, Ellen Sneider, and our two amazing children, Max and Sadie Sneider, without whom nothing else matters. It takes a certain type of personality to launch and run a bootstrapped startup, and a certain type of insanity to write and launch a book while running and growing said business. Living with a hyper-focused, compulsive, maniacal person is not easy . . . I've observed. For them it often means I am not present when I'm present. To correct for this, I'm constantly trying to remind myself that I don't work for me, I work for them. To that end this book, this work, and all my work is dedicated to them.

Contents

Introduction: Are We in the Upside Down? 1

Part I: How to Hack It

Chapter 1: Something Is Broken 15

Chapter 2: Did We Just Reinvent Ad Production? 33

Chapter 3: The Ad Has to Make Money 43

Chapter 4: It's Bigger Than Us 59

Chapter 5: I Get Wild/Wild Gravity 71

Part II: Hacking Advertising

Chapter 6: Hack Creative Production 93

Chapter 7: Hack Your Organization 105

Chapter 8: Hack Client Service 117

Chapter 9: Hack Your Culture 127

Part III: Hacking an Industry

Chapter 10: Hack Your Brand 141

Chapter 11: Hack Your Shop 159

Everyone Asks, "Why Wild Gravity?" 175

Acknowledgments 179

About the Author 181

Introduction

Are We in the Upside Down?

"**W**ait. The agency doesn't make the ads?"

"No."

"Who makes them?"

"The production company."

"So we just spent three months developing the creative with the ad agency," I said, "and they're just gonna hand off the work?"

"They don't hand it off, exactly," my boss replied. "They'll still be there on set. The post-production company will be on set too. They're gonna do all the editing. They want to be on set to mark takes and start ingesting footage. The VFX shop will be on set for this too."

"VFX shop?"

"Visual effects, because we have GPS devices in the spot.

VFX artists will comp in the device screens in post. They need to mark the blank screens for the shoot and make sure the actors use the correct hand gestures on the screens."

"There's going to be another vendor on set to make sure the actor taps on the screen . . . correctly? How many people will be on set?"

"Usually there are around a hundred people, including all the vendors, the talent, hair and makeup, craft services, gaffers, grips, security, and so on. It's quite a production. Literally."

"So we've been working on the ad with twenty-five people, called the 'ad agency,' and they don't actually make the ad?"

"That's right. Well, a bunch of them will be there, like the account team, the creative team, and the agency producers, but sometimes the director of the spot doesn't even want to talk to the agency. You'll have to see what the atmosphere is like there. The account team will be there to take your notes and to make sure you don't talk directly to the director."

"Excuse me?"

"They *really* don't want you to talk to the production people at all during the shoot, especially the director. They'll have a producer you can talk to, and they'll convey all your comments to the director. But really, you're supposed to give all your notes to the account people, who will give them to the agency producer, who will give them to the line producer, who will give them to the director."

"You're telling me the ad-agency-that-doesn't-make-the-ad's

main job once we get to set—*to make the ad*—is to make sure we *don't* talk to the people who are making the ad?"

"Pretty much. You'll give the agency your notes, and the agency will give your notes to the producer, who will run them over to the director."

"Aren't we all going to be in the same place?"

"You'll be in 'video-village' with the agency and a producer, which will likely be in a different room from whatever scene you're shooting. They'll have monitors for you to see the action and headsets so you can hear the dialogue."

"For a scene they're shooting in the next room? Why wouldn't I just stand next to the director and tell him what I think?"

"Yeah, that doesn't happen. And there's not enough room for you and the agency to stand there."

"I wouldn't need the agency right there if I could just talk to the director."

"I love your spirit, but good luck making that happen. It's your first shoot, I'd just go with it. The agency will be great guides for you. Have a great shoot!"

It Shouldn't Have to Be This Hard

This was a conversation between me and my boss at L.L.Bean, right before we went into production on the first television commercial I was in charge of creating. I was director of advertising, reporting to the CMO. All of my previous experience had been in digital marketing. The key difference between a digital agency and a traditional agency is that production in a digital shop is all in-house, since it's just designers and coders. There's no shoot required to launch the new online advertising campaign. I was quickly learning that it was a lot different creating a marketing asset to run on broadcast television.

When I'd been hired, my boss and I had agreed that shooting a TV spot would be just like managing any other project. And it was, in some ways, but there were quite a few differences between digital production and television/video production. Many of these differences seemed to defy the laws of common sense. Little did I know I was just scratching the surface of the absurdities in standard advertising production.

We did end up making a great commercial spot. The director was collaborative with both the agency creative team and with me and my team. We made a New England Christmas spot in Los Angeles. We made snow in Pasadena in July. It was pretty cool . . . for everyone other than the "family" wearing winter clothes and playing in the "snow" in ninety-six-degree heat. They were quite warm.

This would be the first of thousands of television ads and marketing videos I would produce in my career. And as I encountered bigger and bolder professional opportunities, the creative I made became better, bigger, and more challenging (and satisfying) to execute.

After running advertising for L.L.Bean in Maine, I jumped coasts and spent five years as director of advertising for Microsoft

Windows in Washington state. At the height of that position, I had direct oversight of over a quarter-billion-dollar media budget for a Windows launch, and we had the most sought-after, exclusive agencies in the country reporting to us. Literally, the "Agency of the Decade" worked on our account. For lack of a better metaphor, I was first lieutenant, and my boss was the general. I made all the tactical decisions, and she told me if I was right or wrong. I remember when we got our budgets that year, a friend and peer said, "You're gonna laugh when you see the budget number next to your name for the year."

We spent more than half a billion dollars in global media for that launch, and we turned the campaign on in thirty-two countries simultaneously. We took over Times Square for the launch event. We were the first entity ever to take over more than half of the screens in Times Square and have them all synchronized. Adam Levine played a private concert to VIPs at 2 Times Square when we turned the screens on. Bill Gates was there. It was a *big deal*. I told my direct report, "We may never work on anything this big again in our lives." In fact, it was the last big Windows launch for Microsoft.

We almost landed the Red Hot Chili Peppers to do our launch ad. It would've been the first time their music was used in a commercial. Lemmy from Motörhead considered letting us do a riff of "Ace of Spades." Later that year we met Paul Rudd, Rob Corddry, Sarah Silverman, Jennifer Coolidge, Daniel Radcliffe, and Bret McKenzie from *Flight of the Conchords*. I walked the red carpet of the *Walking Dead* season four premier with my wife.

Saw an episode of *American Idol* produced live. Had Damian Kulash from the band OK Go in my office pitching OK Go as artist-in-residence at Microsoft. It was prime time.

I've also seen the view from startup-land. After Windows, I was vice president of advertising and brand at Redfin and led the creation of their first television ad. We worked with a boutique agency and production company. We had a significantly smaller media budget. We launched in four *cities* simultaneously. We did not take over Times Square or make snow in Pasadena. Lemmy was not contacted.

At each stop along the way, I saw different approaches, different budgets, different industries, and different company cultures. But for the most part, from L.L.Bean to Microsoft to Redfin, despite those differences, the ad agency/production house model remained the same. As a result, no matter where I worked, I found myself running into the same problems and inefficiencies that had plagued my first commercial production. For years, I wound up having the same conversations on set, in pre-pro meetings, behind the glass at focus group sessions. *It shouldn't have to be this hard. And it shouldn't have to take this many people!*

It's not like I had some special insight. Everyone in the industry—every marketer, every advertiser, every production person worth their salt—was having the same conversation in the hallways of their workplaces, all asking themselves the same question: Is the agency model broken?

The answer is yes.

Wild Gravity

For more than a decade, I have been compelled to solve the problem of all the bloat and complexity in the advertising production process. I went from working with some of the best and most influential traditional agencies in the industry, delivering for some of the biggest clients in the game, to running my own shop, Wild Gravity—lean, agile, and equally capable of turning over world-class creative for world-class clients. *More capable*, I'd argue.

I realized it's possible to make superb creative that can live on any television or cinema screen with a fraction of the people, timeline, cost, and complexity that the advertising agency process requires. I know how huge brands (and smaller ones) can go to market without burning millions of dollars with advertising agencies.

I want to help brave marketers sick of the agency runaround and all the bureaucratic bullshit to produce the best advertising creative they've ever produced, in the least amount of time, with the least amount of budget and least amount of effort they've ever expended, all while feeling the most control they've ever had over the creative process.

The first thing my company, Wild Gravity does that's different from the traditional advertising production model is to have creative services and production under one roof. We eliminate the most obvious flaw in the advertising production process by having one organization responsible for creative strategy, concepting, production, post-production, visual effects, computer-generated graphics, sound design, and color balancing.

Working through an agency could mean working with separate vendors for almost all of those processes. No wonder agencies need so many account people. That's a lot to manage! But what if it wasn't so difficult? What if it was all under that same roof and took only one producer to manage? Sounds faster. Easier. Simpler, right? From where I'm standing now, I can tell you that it is.

These days, at my own shop, my team has a bias for making things. What we think of, we create. We produce. It forces a practicality of thought that *increases* creativity. Many people assume creativity should have no bounds, but the opposite is true: The best creative comes out of super tight boundaries.

Creatives who work at shops without a production capability will not have that practicality of thought ingrained. Concepts from that shop will need to be vetted for production feasibility within desired budgets. Those concepts might have already been sold to clients, who will now be disappointed that the idea they fell in love with can't be produced. That's just one example. Agencies are idea businesses. They're great at that. They can generate a lot of ideas.

But we're the ones you come to when you're ready to *make something*, you want it to be awesome, and it needs to be done quickly and expertly.

An agency will offer you a tremendous number of services with wonderfully talented people, but they just can't compete with hybrid shops when it comes to turnaround times. I am far from the first one to point this out. This is a well-trodden issue in the ad world. That the ad-production process is broken is widely documented. It has been written about in every major ad publication. It's been the keynote topic at Cannes.

But a lot of people have a lot of money invested in the current paradigm. Billions of dollars. Have you been to Cannes? The industry's reaction is what you would expect. Ad agencies have added production capabilities, and production houses have added agency services.

This gets at part of the problem. Yes, you have the capabilities under the same roof now, but you still have *two separate entities*. You still have years, maybe decades, of processes, habits, and bureaucracy built in. Just because they're in the same building now doesn't mean these entities know how to work together.

I posit that in order to do the hybrid shop correctly, it needs to be built from the ground up. Bolting a production shop onto a giant agency doesn't solve the bureaucracy problem inherent in the traditional agency model.

When creative and production start working together at the concept phase, there is no throwing the work over the wall. The production is baked into the concepts. Nobody is pitching a bunch of work and then thinking about how to get it made after it's selected. We pitch work we know we can make at the budget and timeline required. It's one of the many ways we shortcut the process and save everyone time, money, and effort.

As a client I can tell you, it's not a good look for a shop to come back and say, "You know that concept you loved? We can't make it like we pitched. What if we did it like this?"

We have a lot of sayings around our shop. One of them is "Don't write an elephant into the script if the budget can't support one." If you've got a twenty-five-thousand-dollar budget, an elephant and a wrangler will not be on set, and a VFX artist will not be hired to add the elephant, in post. So, let's not sell the client on one.

It's super common for junior creatives to pitch blue-sky ideas. "Wouldn't it be great if there was an elephant parade and then one of them was picked up by a blimp?" Yeah, it would be great, but it's impossible to execute and we don't have time for that. We need to present ideas that are *actionable*. If you're a creative who works on productions all the time, "Are we going to be able to make that?" is going to be part of your internal editing process, not an afterthought.

In our brainstorms we don't say, "Wouldn't it be cool if we could make this?" We say, "We could make this, and it will be cool." And then we make it.

And now I'm going to tell you how I got here.

PART I

HOW TO HACK IT

Learn the rules like a pro, so you can break them like an artist.

—Pablo Picasso

Chapter 1
Something Is Broken

Every industry has its share of idiosyncrasies and embedded processes that persist despite having no obvious value, and advertising is no exception. Like anything, the longer I spent in the industry, the better I got at my craft. The better I got, the more obvious the inefficiencies of the advertising production process became.

In 2009, my family and I moved to Washington so I could take a job at Microsoft. In less than a year, the best boss I ever had gave me the best opportunity of my corporate career by putting me in charge of broadcast advertising for Windows. From 2009 to 2014, I was director of broadcast advertising, digital advertising, social media, search, and digital video for this multibillion-dollar brand. At the time, Windows was the big dog at Microsoft, with the largest consumer presence (read: biggest budget), and the biggest budget line item was under my name. I was The Man. And my boss was The Woman, a true force of nature who had a better sense of what worked and what didn't work in advertising and media than any other single person I have ever worked with in the industry. In addition, she also commanded a room better than anyone I have ever met. I learned more about the industry in that one position than any I have ever had.

At this time we had the most coveted advertising agency in the country working for us. This is not hyperbole. They had just been named the "Agency of the Decade" by *Ad Age* when we hired them. The first time we met with them, they paraded in with more people than we had chairs for and went through thirty strategy slides and three underwhelming creative concepts, then left. After they walked out, my boss said, "So there's *the agency of the decade.*" Underwhelming is where the relationship started.

Ultimately, I grew to love almost every one of those people who worked on our account (in a work way!), so the talent was clearly there, even if we hadn't seen it at that meeting. This was the first of many cracks I discovered in the foundation of this industry.

How do we prevent this from happening—all over the industry? How do we avoid attending (or hosting) these much-hyped meetings stacked with stellar agency creatives, all amounting to little more than too many people, too many slides, and a *blah* outcome?

The Rhythm of the Business

At Microsoft, our regular campaign production rhythm would follow three campaign seasons: Holiday, Grads and Dads, and Back-to-School. Microsoft's fiscal calendar begins in July and ends in June, so we would usually concept one campaign platform for the fiscal year and vary the messaging for each of the three seasons. All the advertising creative under that platform—all the television, digital, out-of-home advertising, print, and all the other supporting creative—would be developed during three separate, big campaign productions.

We'd spend months with the agency, strategizing on what our campaign platform would be. Once the campaign platform was locked, we would begin to work on all the individual spots. We pretty much only ran :30s and never :60s. We would sometimes cut down :15s from the :30s in the edit, but we only concepted :30s. So we would work until we had about eight to ten proposed spots we felt good about, and then we would test them. Usually, we would make animatics from the storyboards of the ad, and we would use those for focus group testing in markets where we intended to launch the ads. Animatics are what they sound like: a very rough animation of the storyboards, with sound. Not a single person in the industry will tell you that animatics are a good proxy for what the finished ad will look like, but that never stopped any corporation from testing them as if they were finished ads.

We would fly around the world to spend days listening to

regular people that for some reason had nowhere to be on a week-day tell people that did this for a living what was wrong with the ads we intended to make, based on janky animatics.

I remember bemoaning this process during a focus group results meeting one day: "There are twelve people in this conference room that make ads for a living. Why would we listen to twelve people that have free time in the middle of the day and need fifty bucks?"

This was another crack I found.

We would fly from London to Paris to Mumbai to New York to Chicago to . . . Gary, Indiana, with our slapped-together animatics and listen to the least-informed people in the world give us feedback on our ad concepts. Then we'd sum it all up and give it to the agency to make changes, based on this "crucial data source."

The thing about this *crucial data* is that it's all different and conflicting. How did we deal with this? We had an internal research and metrics team at Microsoft that could sort through the feedback to reveal the consistent themes. We could then use the themes that emerged from the feedback as direction for revisions. Sounds reasonable.

It sounds reasonable until you realize that now you're listening to yet another group of people who are not experts in advertising creative, telling you how to optimize advertising creative. So now there are ten to twelve people who are experts in *measurement*, summarizing what ten to twelve groups of ten to twelve people thought about the *animatics* of our ad concepts. How much more removed can you get?

These are thirty-second scripts, mind you. The changes you can make to them are not big. You may end up changing a few words on a few of the scripts, maybe change the demographics on one or two of the lead actors, or change a few of the locations.

Are these changes meaningful? Not at all. Do they make the creative better? One hundred percent no.

If you ask anyone in the industry, they will tell you that advertising creative goes through a feedback loop consisting of multiple rounds of testing, review, feedback, and revisions. And, to a person, they'll tell you that at each stage the creative becomes increasingly watered down, to the point that the end product looks almost nothing like the concept everyone fell in love with at the pitch.

Is It Time to Shoot Yet?

Now, you still haven't shot anything! But it's time to start production. You already know the agency doesn't do that. So the next step is, the agency presents a bunch of different directors who "they like" and are available to direct the campaign.

What this means is that the agency has relationships with several of the big production companies in Los Angeles, New York, and London (and other places obviously, but these are the big three). The production houses each represent a roster of directors. So, the agency selects directors they like, and who are available, from these production houses' rosters.

There's nothing wrong with that process per se, but as the client, you might not know that's how it works. When you hire the director, you're hiring the production company they're attached to. The agency doesn't start with the whole universe of directors for the selection process. They start with: Who are the production shops we like and trust to get the job done? Then, of those directors they represent, which are available on the desired shoot dates? And then from that limited set, the agency will pick who they like for the job.

Now, here's another part of the process that'll make your head explode: You fly down to LA, because even though I mentioned NYC and London, the shoot almost always takes place in LA. So you fly down to LA for the introduction meeting with the director and the production company, and then the director tells you how they envision the look and feel of each spot, the thoughts they have on dialogue changes, alternative lines they'd like to try, and other locations they'd like to explore, and also a different vision for casting.

This director is *a big deal*. They have multiple Super Bowl ads every year. They cost $35K a day. You listen to them. You make the changes.

You fly home and inform everyone back at your giant corporation that you've made significant changes to the creative, based on the feedback of one person. These new changes are informed by none of the data everyone just spent the last month flying around the world to gather. Good times.

It's finally time to shoot! You've locked on talent and locations with the agency, which stays on location with the production company, while you're back on campus defending your team's decision to make more revisions to the concepts based on one meeting with the director versus the minor changes driven by a month's worth of worldwide research.

You fly back down to LA for the shoot, which kicks off with a giant pre-production meeting.

The pre-pro meeting is the most important event in the entire production timeline. It is a giant meeting with the client, the agency, and the production company, led by the director. The client usually has about three to five people in the meeting, the agency might have ten people, and the production company will have a similar number of people, plus the director.

There could be twenty to forty people in the meeting, and our pre-pro meetings would easily last four hours—sometimes all day. In the meeting, you go through the production book, which includes the scripts, schedules, locations, talent, shooting boards, wardrobe, and every other detail of the shoot.

You learn, as the client, that if you don't specifically see something outlined in the pre-pro book and you don't bring it up in the pre-pro meeting, that detail is definitely not going to be in the shoot. Even if it is something you thought was decided weeks ago. If it doesn't make it to the pre-pro meeting, it won't be on film.

Therefore, you have to make sure you cover every detail in the pre-production meeting. *Are we sure we want to use a wheel of cheese for this gag? I thought it was placeholder.* This was an actual question I asked in a pre-pro meeting, prompting a twenty-minute conversation about wheels of cheese. "It's a fun way for kids to get cheese." (Actual quote defending the cheese wheel. Hard to push back on that.)

In general, everyone tends to shoot one spot per day. There was one time in London that we shot two commercials in a day. I don't know why we did it—probably to save some money, which was absurd, considering how much we were spending overall—but we did do it. It took twenty hours, and it was absolute hell shooting the second commercial. That was probably why we chose London. No crew in the US would put up with that. SAG (Screen Actors Guild) would have you thrown in jail. I digress.

We usually shot six to eight spots per campaign. So planning on one spot per day, and including the pre-pro meeting, we'd be on set for a week or two.

This is what a set is like on a commercial shoot for a big brand like Microsoft, with an A-list agency, an A-list production company, and a celebrity director. Almost all our shoots were on location, meaning we usually shot at homes in LA. We did shoot at Universal Studios for one campaign. That was pretty cool, and we shot on a soundstage once, but most of our shoots were on location. As the client, you usually couldn't park at the shoot because all the trucks were parked there.

So, you and your client posse—there's usually two to four

of you—pull up to some random church parking lot and park. There's a food truck ready to make breakfast burritos for you, and there are some agency people waiting for you to arrive. There are specific people at the agency whose main job on set is to hang out with the clients. They're called account people! *Scary.* (Just kidding. I was an account guy when I was agency-side.) On a shoot, the account managers' main job is to hang out with the clients and make sure their needs are being met. And this is key: They manage the communication flow between the agency and the production company.

Ready for this? The client does not talk directly to the production company. Generally, the director comes over to talk to the clients before the shoot day begins and will likely check in a couple times a day. They'll probably be friendly, but by no means is the client to give notes directly to the director during the shoot, even when the cameras aren't rolling. This is strictly *verboten*! Even if they're within earshot.

At the beginning of the day, as the client, you meet up with your account people in the parking lot, you all eat your breakfast burritos, and you all wait for the shuttle to take you up the hill to the house in Pasadena, because for some reason the shoots always seem to be in Pasadena. The whole crew already came through here a couple hours ago, had their breakfast burritos, and have been setting up and getting ready for the first shot.

Anyway, the client/account posse now shuttles up to the house in Pasadena. If you've watched movies, you know what a movie set looks like, and it's exactly the same for a commercial set. It's the full Hollywood experience: Most of the street is blocked off and more than a hundred people are running around. Scaffolding, gear, and lights surround one house, and people with more gear and lights are moving everywhere. It's a hive of activity. There's a craft services trailer with every type of snack and analgesic you could imagine, a bathroom trailer that would slap you in the face if you called it a "port-a-potty," and twenty white-panel trucks. You get escorted to "video-village" by one of the producers, and then you get asked to "approve picture" on the first shot.

Now, this is probably when the director will come over and talk to the clients for the first time and tell you how they see the day going, what to expect, and what they've got set up for the first shot. If there's any question about the set, you might get escorted to it and remain present as the art department repositions the furniture, or whatever it is, to your liking.

Now it's finally time to roll the camera.

I mentioned that the account people are there to manage the communication flow from the client. This is how the feedback loop works on set. The clients, account people, and producer sit on director's chairs in video-village and watch the shots on monitors with headsets on. You kind of murmur to each other if you're liking the takes or not. After the director gets a bunch of different takes from that camera angle, that shot, they'll ask the clients for feedback on it, notes. They want to know from the range of takes if you think any of them would work for the edited spot. If you think so, the crew breaks that shot down and sets up for the next one. If you thought something was off about the takes, or the product wasn't displayed correctly, or any detail was off, you give your notes to the account people. The agency account people give the notes to the production company's line-producer, and then the line-producer runs the notes over to the director, who considers the notes. The director will then give his notes to the first AD (assistant director). The AD gives notes on acting to the actor, notes on lighting to the gaffer, notes on camera to the DP (director of photography), notes on set to the art department, and notes on hair and makeup to . . . *hair and makeup.*

Scene 1. Take 2!

Are you tired yet? We just started shooting!

Throughout the day someone arrives at video-village with the best snacks you've ever had: fresh-made guacamole with ground cayenne and tomato chunks, grilled cheese squares with a ramekin of tomato soup, chilled crab salad on a spinach leaf, fresh-rolled sushi.

In between the snacks, you're approving shots or giving notes on changes. A rhythm starts to develop, and once it does, you break for lunch because you have to. It's a requirement.

Now the crew is so large that even though you've rented out an entire house for the shoot, you need someone else's lawn to set up for lunch. Lunch is from the same food truck that is now set up on the lawn across the street from the shoot. Lunch is unbelievable: a choice of fresh seared oysters, short ribs, or porcini Alfredo. Chocolate lava cake for dessert.

Inevitably during the shoot day, we would end up shooting takes I knew we would end up not using. The more seasoned I got, the more I pushed back on this, and the stranger the answers got on why we were doing takes that we knew wouldn't be used.

We're warming up the actors. We think this could be a lucky-strike extra. Could be web content. One time the global creative director showed up to our shoot and had the actor do a bunch of *angry takes.* For a Windows ad. You know who was angry? I was. You know who else? My boss when I got back from that shoot.

Shoot days are really long and really boring, and re-sets can take a long time. Everyone brings their laptop to work during downtime, but you also walk around. It's at this point that you might notice there seem to be extra people on set that aren't the agency and aren't the production company, but they're also sitting on set behind their own monitors. Who are they?

They are from the post-production company and the VFX company. Two more vendors that are not the agency. Why are they there? The post company is there to start ingesting the footage and, if your bosses want it, to post dailies from the shoot. The VFX company is there to make sure the shots are good for all the VFX work planned for the footage. For Windows and any consumer tech product, this is crucial. It's mostly about making all the screens for the devices, computers, phones, tablets. When you shoot, you shoot with powered-off devices with taped markers on blank screens, and you need to choreograph gestures and movements for the actors to interact with powered-off devices, as if they're on. Later, the VFX company will create and animate the screens and then composite them onto the devices. The screens have to be captured correctly, and the gestures have to match what's going to be happening on the device screen. For any tech product, this is a huge part of the process.

At some point you realize it's way past five. This is not a big deal to you, because you're a salaried employee, but it is a *big deal* on a union shoot. The account people notice you squirming and say, "Hey, can you approve an overage for the shoot day today?" Your mind skips back to all those extra takes you knew you would never need.

At the end of the shoot day, the client/account posse shuttles back down to the church parking lot while the rest of the crew breaks down, and then you all jump in your rental cars, drive back to the hotel in West Hollywood or Santa Monica, and then meet up for drinks and sushi.

After doing this for about a week and a half, almost everybody flies home, and the footage goes to the post house and the VFX shop. The creative leads from the agency stay in LA to shepherd the edit.

The Magic's in the Edit

Once you've done this more than once, you realize it's all about the edit. The person with the largest creative impact is often the editor. For the unseasoned, that's something you may not have even thought about much before the shoot.

Whatever you think you have *in the can*, you realize you had *no idea* until you start to see it cut together. First of all, thirty seconds is short; a ten-hour shoot day is long!

Many of those details everyone stressed over on set are not even in the final spot. Most of the things! Details of the set that provoked arguments are invisible. That scene they got twenty takes on is, of course, not even in the cut. The copy on the screens that took weeks to get approved is not at all legible and flashes on the screen for less than a second.

It can be quite a shock to see the rough cuts for the first time. Often it is quite the *oh shit!* moment. If you're managing the campaign, it's gone through a million rounds of review, you've flown around the world to get feedback on the concepts, and you realize the spots are not going to be close to what was agreed upon—there are a lot of sweaty palms.

Most brands would have rough cuts sent to them by the agency and would then give the agency notes on the cuts. Next, the agency would pass the notes on to the post house. Then the editor would make the changes, then send the changes to the agency, who would again send them back to the client. The process to get to a locked cut could take weeks, with all the back-and-forth.

As mentioned before, my boss was a savant, and she would always have us fly down to the post house for the edit. We would live edit with the agency, in the room, and we would get our spots to near final cut in less than a day.

We didn't say it out loud, but we were already working around the agency in this part of the process. Hashtag foreshadowing.

Guess who is not usually involved in the edit? If you guessed the director, you would've been a step ahead of me the first time around the block. I remember discussing this: "How can the director not be part of the edit, when the whole thing comes together there?" Some directors do edit, others participate, but this is the exception, not the rule.

The Land of a Hundred . . . and One Approvers

Now, when all the notes have been addressed and everyone is satisfied with the cut, you get to a magical stage called "picture lock." Picture lock means no more changes of takes or timing, and now VFX can begin. If you're working for a massive consumer technology brand, this means the animation, tracking, and compositing of screens onto computers, tablets, and phones can start.

That requires VFX artists to re-create screens and behaviors designed and developed by Windows designers, engineers, and developers. They can be rather upset if the product is misrepresented by even a pixel, so this part of the process is quite complex.

The natural question to ask is: Why aren't commercials shot with the devices turned on? There are many reasons shooting screens practically is impractical, but the biggest one is that the screens don't look as good that way. So pretty much everybody puts the screens in during post.

This makes picture lock very important. It is arduous work, getting the screens perfect and getting sign-off from all the engineers, designers, and brand police. If this has happened and the screens have all been "comped in," and then the CMO or CEO reviews it for the first time and wants to change a scene around, that's a big problem.

And it's a big crack in a broken process.

Naturally, everyone wants to get the commercial into as near final shape as possible before the big boss sees and approves it. But what happens if the big boss has a big change?

Well, now it restarts a whole loop. The agency has to take the cuts back to the post house and back to the VFX shop. Picture is no longer locked. Screens may need to be replaced or reanimated.

One note from a CEO will send a ripple from client to agency; agency to post house; agency to VFX shop. Everything is unwound. The game of telephone begins anew.

If it's a universal comment about the campaign, meaning it affects all of your spots, then you can multiply that work by six to eight. Now you're in a world of hurt. You're supposed to be finishing the spots and getting ready to traffic them.

When, finally, all notes are addressed, the commercials look nothing like the concepts, everything is watered down, and everyone has compromised to the point where no one is happy, the campaign launches!

High-five.

This whole process from initial concepting to production to post to trafficking the spots to the networks to air would take three to four months and usually cost about four to six million dollars. We tended to average half a million dollars per spot on production, not counting agency fees. This is industry standard for a traditional production.

We would usually run six to eight ads on-air. In general, a couple of them were *dogs*, meaning they didn't perform by lifting any of the key performance indicators (KPIs) we were measuring, so we'd stop running them right away. Soon enough, the team would optimize down to three or four spots. By about halfway through the campaign it becomes clear to everyone that only one or two of the spots really perform, and you run these to death for the remainder of the campaign.

Now it's a bit of a self-fulfilling prophecy. The KPIs most brands prioritize are: Breakthrough (Do you remember seeing the ad?), Brand Recall (What was it for?), Message Recall (What was it about?), Likeability (Did you like the brand/product?), and Purchase Intent (Do you intend to buy it?). I call these the Five Magic Metrics© because if you nail these five KPIs you will have a successful ad. So, the first three metrics are about memory. The more times you run a spot, the more people will remember it. That's another metric, called "wear-in." If you've been wondering, that's *exactly* why you always end up seeing the same ads on TV over and over again. The brand optimized into those spots and killed all the other ones from the campaign. (For more on the Five Magic Metrics, see the end of chapter 7.)

I've barely scratched the surface of all the work and all the people involved in the standard campaign production process, but doesn't that seem like a cubic buttload of effort and money for two ads that everyone will get sick of? Doesn't it seem like we could do it easier with fewer people? That it would be faster if we did it that way? And higher quality? Wouldn't it even be more *fun* that way?

We thought so too. *Everyone* thought so. My boss and I talked about it all the time. So what did we do?

Chapter 2

Did We Just Reinvent Ad Production?

F irst off, I don't want to seem like I'm trashing ad agencies or saying they add no value. I also want to point out that back when I worked at more traditional shops, we did produce some amazing, beautiful, effective work. The advertising we created with our high-priced agency and partners was indeed world-class and I'm proud to have been a part of it to this day. I'm still friends with many of the agency and production people I worked with to create those campaigns, so there are no people, companies, or even industry sectors to blame—just processes.

In fact, if you didn't work in the industry, you wouldn't even know anything was wrong, other than it seems expensive and slow to produce high-quality commercials. But things were happening in the industry at that point that were making expensive and slow untenable, and now TV was not necessarily the first channel we were shooting for anymore.

As mentioned, I had purview over broadcast and *digital video* for Microsoft, which was essentially just *video* that we made for our digital and social media properties. Some of it was animated, but a lot of it was live action. I had a young woman running multiple video vendors to create the content. She was an ambitious, get-shit-done type of person. I used to joke that she was running a cottage industry out of her office. When I went on a few shoots with her, they looked a lot like our usual TV shoots, just smaller. Fewer people. No craft services. No handmade guacamole. It did *not* look like a Hollywood set. And the videos we got from those vendors were pretty good. Not *amazing*, but pretty good.

Also at this time, we were getting hammered by Apple. The Mac versus PC ads were over, but the Siri campaign was crushing us, and the iPad came out during this period. Apple would release an ad or a video with Siri—verbally kicking us in the nuts—and we would want to release a video in response. I'd call up our expensive amazing agency and say, "I need a video response to this in two weeks." They'd reply, "Well we can get an SOW [statement of work] to you in two weeks."

That wasn't good enough. I started working to develop some of our smaller vendors that worked on digital video to see if we could up the quality from them. I found we could. We made some really cool videos. They weren't broadcast quality, but often the messaging was way more on-point, and the end product was always way more timely and a *lot* less expensive.

I started working with two vendors in particular that became my go-tos. One was a young film-school graduate in Seattle who won a contest we put on to find vendors like him. He had incredible energy and ideas. He and I would riff together, and he would always pull out all the stops to make anything for us. He started his company after I hired him for the first job. To him, we were paying him ridiculous money; for us, it was nothing compared to what we were paying the agency. A little more formal on the agency spectrum was a boutique agency out of LA. With them we did some more prescriptive work.

One of the problems we had with the big, creative agency is they had a very NIH, "not invented here," attitude. And my boss and I had ideas. We were, are, creative. We both had agency chops. I'd call up the big, expensive agency and tell them we had three ads we wanted to make. They would agree to it, but then they would come back with eight different concepts that were similar but not the same as what we asked for.

We tried a little experiment. We brought the two heads of the boutique shop into a conference room in Redmond, and we said, "We have three ads we want to make. They demonstrate the following features and benefits, in what we think is a pretty clever, campaign-able concept." They agreed. And they agreed to do it.

This was such a fun shoot, for a variety of reasons. The first was we were breaking all the rules. We didn't need no stinkin' focus groups! The second was we were shooting with Broken Lizard, of the movie *Super Troopers* fame. Yeah, *those guys*. And they were just as fun to hang out with as you'd think. Paul Soter

(Officer Foster, the meow guy) was the director and is such a sweet, thoughtful guy. We had a great rapport and, unlike working with Big-Huge (our giant agency), I was allowed to talk to him. He *wanted* to talk. We collaborated on the whole shoot. The three spots we shot with them were some of the most fun to make—and the most fun, funny, and *impactful* spots we ever shot at Microsoft.

Here's the best part: Instead of weeks and weeks of pretesting with focus groups and the like, we shot the spots and then put them in-market in our digital channels. All three of those spots cost less to produce than it cost me to produce one spot with Big-Huge. These spots all performed better than the television spots when we ran them side-by-side in our digital advertising channels. We lobbied for and got approval to pull the spots we created with Big-Huge and put the spots we created with Broken Lizard on-air.

Breakthrough

This was really a big moment disguised as a small moment. We had just completely subverted the ad-production process, and nobody realized it until we were on-air. If it sounds like just my boss and I were responsible for making all the ads, *that was not the case*. It takes a village. At a corporation it takes a village. The village was *not* pleased. Put a pin in that.

It was an awakening experience. We were like, "Wait a second here." I remember talking to the CEO of the boutique agency and my boss at Windows and saying, "I think we just backed into the new model." We concept, shoot, edit the spots, and then we "test them" in-market in our digital channels. The best-performing spots in digital we air on broadcast. It was sounding pretty smart. Pretty efficient. Everything tested in-market. No focus groups. Rather than test animatics before an expensive production, we could run a much less expensive production and then test the actual creative in-market in digital channels. It made so much more sense.

We were going to be able to do it! We were going to be able to fire Big-Huge and put in the new model! We were going *to reinvent advertising.* We were going to be all over *Adweek* and *Ad Age.* We would be darlings (or villains!) at Cannes. It. Was. Happening!

Enter New CMO. New CMO was a big player in the political world. He basically invented overnight polling and message testing and was responsible for getting many big-name politicians elected. Interesting guy to come in as your boss's new boss. Working with him was one of the strangest experiences of my career and would eventually lead to me leaving Microsoft. But I'm getting ahead of the story.

Another thing to know about New CMO is he basically invented the attack ad and was a big advocate of *going negative.* As you might suspect, this is a better strategy for a net-zero game like political campaigns and not usually a recommended strategy for brand advertising.

By this point, we had won the approval to create a full campaign with our darling boutique agency but, unfortunately, we couldn't protect the campaign from getting corporatized. Meaning we did have to go through the around-the-world focus group testing with our animatics. We did have to go through all the other rigamarole. We used an A-list production company and a big director. The boutique agency was thrilled they were going through that whole process. For them it was like putting on their big-boy pants. And, like wary parents, my team and I felt as if we were watching our innocents get bespoiled. And what suffers in the end? The creative.

Sure enough, at the end of the production the spots we produced were good, high-quality commercials, but they looked little like the concepts we'd fallen in love with at the pitch. It was as if the process itself *wouldn't let go*. Our darling was corrupted in the first go-round. *C'est la* corporate advertising.

When we were in creative development, New CMO came into one review and said the dialogue wasn't authentic enough. I remember standing outside in the rain on my phone at the end of the day, asking my boss in desperation, "Why are we letting the guy that makes inauthentic attack ads tell us what's authentic?"

The most surreal meeting of my corporate life was the follow-up meeting. My boss, a colleague, and I went over to present new, *more authentic* scripts to New CMO at the executive building. It was a 6:00 p.m. meeting and unfortunately our scripts, written by our beloved agency, did not pass the New CMO test. "Not authentic enough." What to do? Well, New CMO told us he used to work on *The West Wing* as a consultant. "Why don't I get my writer friend on the phone to work with us?" At that point, I had to "brief" the writer from *The West Wing* over the phone to rewrite the scripts—ones we were about to go into production with, by the way—so they would be "more authentic." We worked with him until ten at night rewriting the scripts.

The next day, he sent us incredible scripts full of character development, flaws, successes. Aaron Sorkin–level work. And length. If our thirty-second ads were able to be twenty minutes long, then these scripts would've been fantastic. So, we made a few token changes to the scripts we already had and went into production.

The end result was a campaign that looked nothing like the original concepts we all loved. The creative was watered down from focus-group testing and was off-tone due to mandatory changes based on executive whims. Of course, executives would never see it that way, so our experiment was deemed a failure, and it was clear to management that smaller shops were not the answer—and in fact the new thinking was that Big-Huge was not big or huge enough, so New CMO hired the biggest-hugest agency in all the land. For real.

Things Get Spicy

In the end, while we'd all been really excited, we shouldn't have been surprised. This was a giant corporation, after all. There was an entire organization within Microsoft whose entire job was to manage the agencies. They demanded to be the direct interface with all of our agencies-of-record, and we had to run all of our agency communications through them. And of course, we felt we didn't need them and wanted to run our agencies directly. To say that was a politically fraught stance was putting it mildly.

The CMO for Microsoft sat in the central marketing organization. We were in the business group. This was all connected to a larger power struggle over who controlled advertising for Windows, which at the time was the tail that wagged Microsoft.

In the wake of our inspiring experiment, business continued on with multiple vendors. The business group and the central marketing group worked on the main campaigns together with Big-Huge, and my team, which was only two to three of us, worked on "digital video" with our smaller, funner [*sic*] vendors. We kept giving them bigger budgets and better briefs, and things were getting *spicy*.

Then, something shifted. There was a giant reorg in the works. The centralized marketing team was disbanded, and the CMO (no great fan of our team) got a huge separation package and was no more. Suddenly, that big rival organization was going to be assimilated into our group.

While I had always told myself that I had the best job at Microsoft, in the back of my mind I knew it wouldn't last forever. Too many people wanted my role, and I wasn't political. As soon as I saw the sands were shifting, I started looking around and I heard about a vice president of advertising job at Redfin.

I threw everything I had into landing that job. It was the most intense hiring process I've ever been through, involving, among other things, developing a presentation and presenting it to the entire executive team as a group and interviewing with every one of them one-on-one. The process went on for weeks, and it was grueling. The whole time, the CEO was saying, "I want to hire you, but I'm not sure what the team's going to say."

Somehow everything aligned. The reorg on our team at Microsoft was complete, and my boss scheduled a meeting for the two of us at the pub near campus. At this point I had worked for her for seven years: two years at Fidelity in Boston and five years at Microsoft. I had an idea what we were going to talk about. She started to explain that I was going to get "layered"— meaning I would have a senior executive inserted between me and her.

I said to her, "Nah, I'm not gonna do that." She looked at me, puzzled. I told her about the new gig. She laughed and gave me a big high-five. "Thank God. I knew you weren't going to like that." She remained an invaluable confidante, but we parted ways, workwise—for the time being.

And it was on, on, on to the next one.

Chapter 3

The Ad Has to Make Money

I started a new job as vice president of advertising and brand at Redfin. I was beyond excited. This was my first executive title. I had been at the director level at my last three jobs, which was cool and all, but V-to-the-motherfuckin'-P: I was psyched. In addition, this was a pre-IPO startup at a time when startups would go public and explode. I was thinking, *I'm going to be at the same level, stature-wise, that my boss was in but in a growing, hot startup.*

What made the job particularly compelling was that they were starting work on their first television ad, and I was to helm the project. Now that I had learned that it was possible to create world-class advertising creative with a fraction of the resources and timeline required by the standard ad agency process, I was excited to build the infrastructure and implement this process at a sizable, growing startup. I was thinking, man, are they going to be psyched when I show them how to do this faster, easier, cheaper, and better.

Before that happened, I knew I had to come in and gain everyone's trust and prove that I could deliver. Before I started, the executives had hired a boutique ad agency and begun creative development of the TV commercial I was to shepherd to completion. I was to come in and take over that project and work with the agency and production company to produce their first spot.

They were using a traditional agency production model, and this was right in my wheelhouse—I had done this hundreds of times by this point. I knew that I could crush it (and I did). I helped to finalize the script and concept and took over management of the production. My official start date was about two weeks before the shoot date.

I was psyched that I was coming in to do what I loved right off the bat. I kind of felt like the special-ops guy coming in to lead the company to a new stratum. My plan was to come in and deliver this spot, then build out the above-the-line advertising capability at Redfin. I was going to show them how to completely flip the script on advertising production.

After I delivered this first spot, I was going to show them how they could do it again—faster, better, and cheaper.

I thought my boss, the CEO, was going to be thrilled to learn all this stuff. He was a big fan of hacking systems and doing things DIY. If we wanted to do a survey, we wouldn't hire a vendor. We would write the survey ourselves and put it on Survey Monkey. We had internal search-engine marketing and optimization (SEM/SEO) capabilities. Online advertising, social media, and all the below-the-line capabilities were in-house, lean, mean, and pro.

Redfin is a smart company. Best dataset in real estate. If you're looking for a house, you should be on Redfin. It's a very math-oriented company. What was interesting was that on this first shoot, despite a few peculiarities, the process looked almost identical to the one we used at Microsoft. It was pro, but in no way was it lean and mean.

They had hired a midsize independent agency out of Marin County, California, that was well established in the industry. The agency, in turn, had hired one of the production companies out of LA that I had worked with many times before. It felt just like another Microsoft shoot.

I ran the shoot in LA, and we made a really nice spot for Redfin's first real TV ad. What I would call a base hit, straight up the middle. Not a home run by any means. But it was a perfect brand-building, value-prop-establishing spot.

Redfin's problem, as I characterized it, was a marketer's dream: People loved the product/service, but not enough people knew about it. This is a great problem to have because it's easy to solve. You just need to drive Awareness, Brand Recall, and Message Recall. Easy. The spot did that really well. And it looked gorgeous. I'm still super proud of it.

We'll Know It's Working If the Phone Rings

The trouble began when I got back to Seattle after shooting the ad. We were in an executive status meeting with our Redfin CEO. There were about six VPs plus the CFO and CEO, and I was presenting our measurement plan for the ad.

I started explaining: We're going to run the spot in four markets (cities). We've found four like-markets, cities with similar sizes and demographics, where the spots won't run. We're going to run brand surveys before and after the spots run in all eight of those markets. We should be able to get a clear read on what brand metrics the ad drove from—

"Why are we going through so much trouble to measure the ad?" the CEO said, interrupting my presentation. "We'll know if the ad works if the phone rings."

"Excuse me?" I asked.

"We'll know if the ad works or not if the phone rings or it doesn't."

I was sweating. Everyone was looking at me. I was new, about a month in now, just back from my first big project, which was a massive investment for this company. *Based on his statement*, I thought, *does he not understand the strategy of the creative?* We didn't create an ad to "make the phones ring."

"Well, first of all, there's no phone number on the ad," I started. "I think you know that."

"Oh I know, I was just being metaphorical. We'll know if it's working if we get a lot of web-hits in that city."

"Well, that would be a leading indicator," I said. "But I just want to be clear on what the objectives of the ad were: to drive brand awareness and message recall. We agreed very specifically that this is a *brand ad*. What you're talking about is measuring the effectiveness based on *direct marketing* metrics. Now, I could make you a direct marketing ad, but I don't think you'd like it. It would have a lot of 'call now,' 'visit now,' 'how much would that be worth to you' type of messaging, and I don't think that's on-brand for Redfin."

"I know it's a brand ad, but we need to know how much money it makes so we know if we're going to do it again."

"What?"

"If it doesn't make money, we're not going to do it again."

"Brand advertising doesn't really work like that," I said. "It's not a switch that you turn on and off. You start running an ad and it takes a while for it to wear-in, and metrics will improve for a long time before you see wear-out. What you want to do is stack messages, to grow brand metrics. It's going to be a bit of a waste to turn an ad on for a few months and then just stop advertising."

"Well, you're going to need to prove that it made money if we're going to do this again."

Holy fuck, my new job was imploding in the first exec status meeting! I thought I was being brought in to help develop a new advertising capability for them. In my CEO's mind, this one commercial was a trial, and if it "didn't work," they weren't going to make another one. I was freaking out.

Also, this issue was the holy grail of ad measurement. People have been trying to solve this since John Wanamaker famously said, "Half the money I spend on advertising is wasted; the trouble is I don't know which half."[1]

Return on investment (ROI) or return on ad-spend (ROAS) for a direct-response ad is easy to prove because you use a unique vanity phone number or URL, so you know exactly how much business you drive. You can also use a coupon or a discount code to track responses. But if you're not using any type of direct-response mechanism, it's extremely difficult to get to an accurate ROI or ROAS. Especially if you're not selling a retail product.

In this instance, the commercial was designed to drive *awareness* of Redfin. It's reasonable to assume that more people would search for the brand and that there would be a corresponding increase in home searches. However, in no way would money be trading hands the day the ad launched. The sales cycle of home buying and selling is long (it could take a year or two to find the right home), so it's not as if you could measure the dollars

---

1 George Bradt, "Wanamaker Was Wrong—The Vast Majority of Advertising Is Wasted," *Forbes*, updated September 14, 2016, https://www.forbes.com/sites/georgebradt/2016/09/14/wanamaker-was-wrong-the-vast-majority-of-advertising-is-wasted/.

an ad was driving in the same way you could if you were selling consumer goods.

It's such a hard problem that at Microsoft there were well over a hundred people on the metrics team. It was a similar issue with Windows, where you're marketing an operating system that runs on machines your company doesn't make, sold at stores you don't own.

Also similar to home sales, computer sales tend to be driven more by macroeconomic factors, seasonality, and life-step changes than by deals or ads.

Due to that, we looked at every different KPI there was to use as a proxy for revenue so we could know how our campaigns moved the market. After looking at Brand Recall, Message Recall, Likeability, and all the other likely factors, Purchase Intent (PI) had the closest correlation to sales, unsurprisingly. When we examined past sales data, bumps in PI correlated with bumps in demand when corrected for macroeconomic factors.

That kind of makes sense, right? But it's a complicated concept to convey to convince someone that *their ad is making money*. For example, it's hard to tease out how much revenue was driven by a two-point bump in purchase intent.

I couldn't simply measure purchase intent and call it a day. We weren't *selling houses* in the ad; we were driving awareness of the brand and offering. Nonetheless, my boss made it my mission to develop a methodology that would measure the ROI by market of the commercial we had just made—by the week.

Somehow, I needed to develop a proxy model based on past data that was going to tell us if the ad was making money or not, based on whatever KPIs turned out to be the best correlation to revenue for Redfin.

There wasn't an immediate answer in-house. It was going to take analysis of dozens of different factors like web traffic, tour-booking rates, offer submission rates, and other metrics that I would have to prove were a good proxy for future revenue. And I didn't need to just show a correlation—it had to have a dollar amount attached to it. It needed to be so concrete that we could say something like "every home tour booked is worth X dollars in future revenue," in order to calculate real-time ROI metrics for the ad that executives and board members would find credible.

I had to shelve the brand-measurement methodology I had developed with the media agency and now had to develop a home-brew, direct-response methodology with the metrics and analytics team at Redfin.

Mind you, I'd been at this job for about a month and had gone to LA for the first week to shoot the spot. As the vice president of advertising and brand, I'd inherited a team of twenty people, and I was responsible for brand, Redfin.com, all the collateral, brokerage advertising, broker photography, real estate photography, and about a zillion other things. So now on top of all my everyday leadership responsibilities, I had to find the holy grail of ad measurement as an individual contributor, as if that were my full-time job—all while being inundated as an executive. It was a serious environment. They were getting ready to

IPO (initial public offering), so we had *serious* board meetings. I had to present to a board for the first time. I had to manage multiple teams, scores of projects, and then I had this side gig of solving advertising measurement. *No big deal.* I was deeper in spreadsheets than I had been since Stats II in grad school.

Not only this, there was also a whole team of people at Redfin who did this for a living. They were analysts. They were metrics people. They were numbers people. I mean, I got my MBA. I can run simulations on Excel if I have to, but it's not my thing. I didn't choose to do that for a living. Suddenly, however, I was forced to take on this Herculean task that was not my forte at all—in a silo. And I had to prove the efficacy of the job I'd just been hired to do.

I thought I had been hired to build an advertising capability. Now I had to prove that *advertising worked.*

I was freaking out. The job was overwhelming in many ways. Several of my peers were like therapists for me. I was asking, "Is this a test? Why is he having me do this when it's clearly not my expertise?" Nobody was sure exactly. For the most part my days were spent leading the advertising and brand team, but then I had this side gig of proving the worth of my existence. That's what it felt like, anyway.

Wear-out

But guess what? I did it. I ended up delivering a methodology to measure the ROI for the ads in each of the four cities they were going to run in: Boston, Seattle, San Francisco, and Austin. This was a huge investment for the company; the media is of course a huge part of the budget. If you've managed your advertising budget well, it should be the largest part of your budget—by a lot.

My boss had me develop all these cutlines for when we would pull the ad if it wasn't performing well enough in any given market. So at four weeks, it had to be at X level and at six weeks it had to be at Y level.

All this time I was telling him, "It's a brand ad; it's meant to drive brand metrics, not sales directly. The way brand advertising works is you start running ads in a market and it needs to wear-in before your key metrics start to rise. The first thing is Breakthrough. If you don't break through, no other metrics matter."

It takes so much repetition that at Windows-level media spending, it would take a few weeks for our ads to start to reach any meaningful level of breakthrough. It's called wear-in when that happens, which really just means that people are starting to remember the ad.

"Wear-out" is when breakthrough stops growing and other metrics start declining. Essentially, people get sick of it. We never, ever got to wear-out with a Windows ad. That's not a flex; it just takes a lot of repetition to get there. We, internally, would just move on to a new campaign. I used to joke that our ads reached "executive wear-out." *We* got sick of them.

Cognitive Dissonance

I continued to make the case to my new boss that the best way to maximize the investment in this really nice piece of creative would be to run it as much as possible. *Run it, run it, run it.* Every time you run it, it becomes a better investment. It both amortizes the initial investment in the production budget and increases the efficacy of the ad. Meaning your KPIs are going to keep getting higher for a long time.

I kept trying to explain this, and I kept saying the smartest thing to do would be to follow it up with another spot in a few months and then develop a rhythm, so it could become a recognizable campaign and, eventually, a beloved brand.

"I very much want all that to happen, but if the ad's not making money four weeks in, we're going to pull it" is the answer I got.

At this point I feel obligated to point out that the advertising agency had been hired only to make this one television ad. They didn't make anything else for Redfin. No print ads, digital ads, collateral, nothing else. They went through an extensive onboarding process. They did their strategy sessions. Their big brand-planner presentations. All of it. I hadn't been there for these, but I'd seen the decks and all the invoices. The agency fee for the year was just north of three-quarters of a million dollars.

The agency did not make the ad. You already know this.

Redfin had hired a production company—one I had already worked with, with Big-Huge. So that spot cost around three-quarters of a million as well, all-in with production, post, VFX, finishing, and music.

So, more than one and a half million dollars to make one thirty-second spot that was . . . pretty good. I mean, it was good. I'm proud of it, but I've produced much better creative for a lot less money.

We were way off on our creative/media ratio, especially if we pulled the ad after four weeks. What was especially strange about this was that Redfin was extremely cost-conscious and always looking for efficiencies in other arenas. As I mentioned, they ran search-engine marketing and online advertising in-house and had positive ROI. (Note: It's a lot easier to track ROI for digital marketing.)

I thought, *Here's my chance to come in and show him I'm the real superhero.* I was like (sic), "Hey, you know how we spent one and a half million to produce that one ad? I'm going to show you how we can produce three ads for half a million that are all better than that one."

"Not interested."

"What?"

"Let's just see how this ad goes."

"Wouldn't you at least want to meet one of the production shops I've worked with? They're right here in Seattle, and we've made award-winning television creative together."

"Fine."

I bring my Redfin CEO and my colleague, the VP of PR,

who is great and was a great confidante while I worked there, to visit this shop in Seattle. The founder of this shop was the filmmaker I'd hired at Windows, and the meeting was in this gutted old building in Seattle that they were renovating at the time. It was down to the studs, but he was super passionate about how his team was going to renovate the building. There were going to be twenty-foot ceilings, exposed brick, four client-facing edit suites, a half-court basketball court, ten VFX bays . . .

My CEO was unimpressed. We went down to a conference room and got the full pitch, saw some beautiful work, including a bunch of stuff he and I had shot together when he was a solo filmmaker and I was his client at Windows. We showed the Redfin CEO the award-winning commercial that he and I had produced in less than a month from brief to on-air called "Empowering Women." We had made it for Bing in time for New Year's Eve after getting the brief on December fourth, which was essentially: "We need a New Year's Eve ad." We won a Gold Telly Award for it. People *cried* when they watched it. We had made it for about fifty grand. My boss was still not impressed.

Not only that, when I saw him at the office the next day, he was low-key mad at me. At this point I asked him, "It seems like you're mad at me. What's up with that?"

"Well, I don't understand why you're wasting my time showing me your friend's space. It's clear that he never sang for his supper."

"What? I'm trying to show you that when—okay, if—we're ready to make more TV spots, there's a much more inexpensive way to produce them that looks just as good, if not better."

"That was just a waste of all three of ours' time at this point."

"Wouldn't it be meaningful to our ROI calculations if our ad production investment was lower?"

"Yeah, well, you're a long way from proving if this first ad is even gonna work."

Touché.

Seriously?

Around this time I got a text from the now former CEO of the darling boutique agency I had hired when I was at Microsoft. Since then, he had started a new content marketing company with two other people. They were about six months in. Would I be interested in coming on as an executive?

Well, let me think about that!

It was still pretty early in this Redfin job—I was six months in. Despite feeling like I was often fighting for my existence, I was also getting into the groove on this job. My team had redesigned the website. We redesigned all the collateral. I had been told by the CEO, "Don't even try to redesign the yard sign; it's so politically fraught it's a loser of a project." But I worked with three talented designers on my team to redesign the yard sign despite the warning. I *was* able to land it. Everyone loved it. If

Redfin is in your area, the yard signs you see today were created by that little team I led. I had a lot of successes in a short time, so I was starting to get my footing.

I was hitting my stride in many ways. I presented at *Redferno*! This was the annual gathering of Redfinnians, which was all of corporate, plus all the real estate agents. It was a big sales pump-up fest. I presented to five thousand people, which was the biggest audience I've ever presented to by far. My boss said I killed it, and you know by now that he didn't just dole out compliments. I'm still proud of it, as you can tell, so it wasn't like my job was a *total* nightmare. There were just nightmare parts of it.

I started talking to my buddy, the one who'd just started the content marketing shop. "Would you guys be willing to make me CMO?" I asked. *Yes.* "I could start an office here in Seattle?" *Yes.* "You could match my salary?" *Yes.* "And a 5 percent commission on gross for accounts I open?" *Yes.*

Hmmm . . . that could be pretty interesting, and lucrative. And I'd get to work with people I really liked versus muddling through the twilight zone I was in now. What was there to think about?

When we finally had the model all worked out and the media fine-tuned, we launched Redfin's first ad ever in four cities—and guess what happened? It was a hit! It blew out all the metrics on the model I built. It made money! *I had done it.*

There was a lot of excitement around the office. I was psyched. Gave myself a high-five. Then, a few weeks into the campaign, my peer in charge of metrics and operations sent a letter to all of us on the senior leadership team to the effect of:

> The television ad is overperforming in two of the four markets and our representatives cannot meet the demand, so I've informed the media department to stop running the ad in those markets.

I sent a one-word email to my boss: "Seriously?"

He asked what I would do in this situation, were I him. Let's just say we disagreed about tactics on how to handle the demand. Over the next few weeks I made a recommendation for, ran the search, and secured a new direct-response television agency for Redfin.

I gave notice about a month later.

Chapter 4

It's Bigger Than Us

'd thought Redfin was a startup. No, *this* new gig was a startup. I'd flown down to LA as soon as I started. Their office was in the basement of the *Los Angeles Times* building, which was a weird building—really cool in many ways. So much history. Front pages were hung up and down all the hallways. Everything was original Art Deco.

Also, there were about a tenth of the number of people in the building than it was designed to hold because . . . *internet.* Everyone knows that story.

But because print media was getting decimated, office space in the *LA Times* building was super cheap for our startup. We literally were new media replacing old media.

Going into the office there was going subterranean in an old, cool, ghost-town building. Kind of cool. Kind of creepy. The office itself had wires hanging from the ceiling, paper everywhere, people running around, phones ringing—the quintessential busy startup. The energy was great. I loved it. The mess was part of the charm.

This was an environment where I could move my story forward. At Microsoft I felt like we had developed a new way to go-to-market without all the agency BS. In my mind, that boiled down to these things:

- Agency services, production, and post-production all under one roof

- Small teams of senior talent

- Removal of all traditional agency processes not directly related to driving impactful creative

- Leveraging efficiencies to develop better work, faster and for less money

A massive part of the appeal of going to this shop was that they were implementing the model I had been preaching—the hybrid shop with agency services, production, and post-production all at the same location.

These guys shot everything, edited, created all the motion graphics, VFX, and so on. They owned all their own equipment, and everyone was an expert at what they did. Everyone had agency chops. There were only about thirty-five people there, but they could churn out gorgeous, high production-value work faster than any ad agency and production shop ever could.

There was another interesting layer here. Their first client was Bud Light at the time Bud Light was doing that "Whatever, USA" campaign. If you don't remember it, Bud Light would come into a town and turn the entire town into a Bud Light summer camp for adults. Everything—every street, store, sign, and so on—was painted blue and branded for Bud Light.

It was like a festival and a summer camp for twentysomethings mixed into one. The first one was in Crested Butte, Colorado, and the second on Catalina Island in California. I started working for the company in between the two events.

The way this campaign worked, there were Bud Light photo booths in bars around the country where consumers auditioned to go to Whatever, USA. They had to "prove" that they were "up for whatever." If they were selected, Bud Light would pay for their travel and lodging for the two-day Whatever, USA, fest. Winners wouldn't know exactly where they were going or what would happen. They just had to clear their schedule for that weekend, choose a couple of friends, and go. There were surprises in store for the winning contestants. If they were an up-and-coming rapper, they might meet Lil Jon or Snoop Dogg. A rookie MMA fighter would meet Ronda Rousey. And so on.

This was all for the purposes of generating great content. These people were filmed every step of the way. Not only that—we had editors and VFX artists on site with us. We were cutting this content into finished commercials overnight and trafficking them the next morning for digital distribution. The turnaround time was unheard of.

Soon, Bud Light was able to generate enough content from one two-day live event to fill their entire media calendar for a campaign season. All of their TV, digital, social—all of it. They didn't have to shoot any "ads," and it was so much faster, so much cooler, so much more engaging. Talk about skipping the agency. This was skipping that whole process altogether.

Really, it was changing the nature of the shoot from something concepted by the agency that was then acted out and filmed, to an event with real people where nobody knew exactly what was going to happen, and the creative part happened during the production and the edit.

We sat at the same table as the agency-of-record in the Bud Light vendor status meetings. Boy, did they hate this campaign. Bud Light didn't give a fuck. Interesting tidbit: Everyone in Bud Light marketing tends to be in the same demo as the target market, so early twenties. InBev, the parent company, moves them on to new jobs fast, so these young execs tend to take risks and also tend not to be business-relationship conscious. They didn't care how the agency felt. They were thinking, *This is cool. Let's keep doing it!* So we did.

Whatever, USA

I started right before the Catalina Island shoot. The whole operation was super impressive. I met Ronda Rousey. She was the champ then, and we shot a spot where she met a young female MMA fighter who had no idea Ronda would be there.

We filmed a spot with Snoop Dogg. Funny story: Catalina Island, if you don't know, is just off the coast of LA. We take a boat there. Snoop and his posse chopper in from the city way too close to the start time of the set he's supposed to put on. They roll up in blacked-out Suburbans and immediately pour into this house we're using as a greenroom. They're there for a really long time. A few crews are waiting to shoot bits with him before he does his set. The thing is, the D-O-double-G is on his own time frame.

First, we hear: "Snoop has to get high first." Everyone kind of chuckles and shares knowing looks, like, *How classic is this?*

Then: "Snoop is now too high to come out." Nervous chuckles at this. There are a couple of film crews, journalists, and he's got a concert to give kind of soon now. So everyone wonders if Snoop is going to do all the bits and interviews he's scheduled for. People have been waiting for three or four hours by this point.

One of his drivers pipes up, "Listen! I've seen this a million times. He's gonna come out. You're all gonna get what you need."

Soon enough, Snoop emerges with his lady and a massive spliff. He has one more puff, hands off the joint, and nails all the bits in single takes. We have an up-and-coming rapper whose dream is to meet Snoop. The kid is loving it. Everyone ends up being thrilled. Snoop overdelivers for everybody.

Then, he goes down to the stage to put on one of the best hip-hop sets I've ever seen live. He wraps the set, heads back to the chopper, and he's out. It probably takes him all of three hours to do the whole thing from LA and back, and he absolutely kills it for everybody.

I am dumbstruck. Damn, is that guy a *pro*. Beyond impressive. Yeah, the guy smokes a ton of weed. He's also one of the most professional, dependable entertainers in the industry. Snoop is no fucking joke. I have such massive respect for him after seeing him deliver like that.

Why tell that story? Snoop delivers high-end creative on super-tight timelines using a small group of pros. He delivers faster than industry standard, so people aren't even expecting it and they build in extra time. But because Snoop is such a seasoned pro, he can deliver on a dime. It was another lesson I tucked away for later.

We made some amazingly cool content through that campaign platform. That was just one of the scores of spots we made from that event. And. The most important thing for advertising, you now know, is breakthrough. It broke through.

It didn't look like other stuff on TV. The spots had a ton of energy. The people in them weren't actors pretending to have fun. The spots looked fun, because *it had been fun*. It made people who saw those ads, who looked like the people in the ads, want to go to their local bar to try out for the next one. It really was an ingenious campaign.

I remember my friend—the CEO—and I had dinner together and we were talking about it. This is the same guy who had been

CEO of the boutique agency we used when we shot with Broken Lizard. We had had conversations about this new ad production model on that set years before. (Everything's connected!) We were implementing the model we had concepted on that Windows shoot years ago. Here was the model, working better than we had ever imagined. I remember him saying to me, "It's bigger than us, Jon." I thought he was being corny at the time, but he was right.

At the time, I was thinking, *It's not bigger than us; it is us.* I was so passionate about this. I called up my old colleagues at Microsoft and was able to get us registered vendor status right away, which is almost unheard of. And then I started booking pitch meetings for us all over Microsoft.

Our pitch was really good. The content was really good. We landed projects. Microsoft started sending us work, and I started looking for office space near my house and near the Microsoft campus. It was surprisingly expensive for just a few people, even for a WeWork-type setup, if you wanted to have any type of an "office" that could expand. We wanted more than a couple of cubbies.

I noticed that residential properties were cheaper per square foot where I was looking. I found a three-bedroom apartment in a complex on Lake Washington, with access to a conference room that none of the tenants used, and a theater we could use for presentations. Our executive staff could stay in the bedrooms instead of hotels when they came up for meetings at Microsoft. Sold!

We were reinventing every model. What could go wrong?

Couple things. Remember that cool Bud Light campaign and the twentysomething marketers who rotated through that didn't give a fuck about the agency's feelings? Well, they rotated through, and there were now new twentysomething marketers who didn't care about *our* feelings and really liked getting wined and dined by a Big-Huge agency. They were super impressed by all the strategy slides and the requisite British brand-planner. So, that groundbreaking new model that was bigger than us, that *was* us? It was gone.

The Writing on the Wall

Something you should know about AB InBev, the corporation that owns Budweiser, should you ever start your own shop, is that they pay their invoices Net 180. Net 180 is pretty much unheard of. It means they pay their vendors six months after the invoice is submitted. For reference, most corporations pay Net 30 or Net 60, and Net 60 is painful for a small shop. If you own a business, just reading the words "Net 180" makes you sweat. Net 180 can literally put you out of business, and that's what they're counting on.

AB InBev saves millions and millions of dollars by letting small vendors go out of business before the check is due. To rub salt in the wound, when our six months was up, instead of paying the bill, they started an audit of the job. This included time cards from a shoot now over six months ago, shot on Catalina

Island, where we had multiple teams running twenty-four hours a day. I think it took another three months to get that sorted and get paid. We got paid about ten months after the job was done and that gig was over.

That didn't affect me directly, but it did drive significant layoffs in LA, and it was something that stuck with me when it came time to build Wild Gravity.

It also put a big damper on our *this is the new model!* enthusiasm. I mean, we still said it, but that definitely took wind out of our sails.

Now along with layoffs, our small office in Seattle started getting creative back from LA that suddenly didn't look as good. We would get round-two cuts with a lot of the client notes unaddressed, the color looking flat, or without that extra drone shot.

The quality was slipping because staff numbers were down, and the morale was down with the remaining staff, so nobody was psyched to go the extra mile.

When I had accepted the job, I had told my friend, the founder, "The one thing I'm nervous about is that you guys will sell too fast." They had granted me 1 percent shadow equity, which meant I would get the value of that if/when they sold, but I didn't actually have any equity rights. If they sold for $5 million I'd get $50K. Not huge money. I had walked away from a few million in potential stock options from Redfin, so I was hoping that they would hang on for a while to see if maybe the model caught on and we could sell for significantly more than that.

Well, they got an offer almost right away. Within two months of me signing on with them, the events company that created Whatever, USA, asked the three founders if they would entertain a bid. I started freaking out.

I was told not to worry. I would have designated "key man" status in the contract as part of the deal. That would ensure that the purchasing company would keep me on after the deal closed. I was assured, "You're the only one in the contract besides us. So your job should stay the same, but you'll have more resources and a steady revenue stream." It didn't make me feel better.

All of the above did not happen in order, and it was not nearly as succinct in the living of it as it is in the retelling of it. Everything was cascading on top of each other with a myriad of other complicating factors. We soldiered on. The deal closed. The parent company asked me to write down all of my Microsoft contacts. I laughed and laughed.

I, of course, knew exactly what was going to happen. The purchasing agency didn't care about our new model. They did care about my Microsoft account. That account was a big reason why they'd bought the company. They already *had* a CMO. I saw the writing on the wall. I had seen it as soon as I'd heard about the bid.

I did all the work the purchasing agency asked me to. They had me co-pitch Johnsonville Sausage with them in Milwaukee—myself, their CMO, and their ECD (executive creative director). The three of us drove from Milwaukee to Johnsonville, Wisconsin, to pitch to the Johnsonville Sausage execs. Our CMO introduced us, and I co-pitched with the ECD. It was a good pitch. He had too many slides. Don't tell him.

If you were wondering, the meeting was a total *sausage party*. Not one woman on the executive team. One hundred percent sausage.

Those same guys came into town for a bunch of Microsoft meetings they had me set up. For some reason my most valuable contacts never seemed to be available (wink). I did the work they asked for, but I never did write down that list of contacts.

The day came soon enough. My role was eliminated.

As part of the key-man clause, I had a six-month severance package. I was already thinking, *If I could get Microsoft as a client for them, I bet I could get Microsoft as a client for me.*

Chapter 5

I Get Wild/
Wild Gravity

thought long and hard about applying for senior marketing roles at Microsoft, or Amazon, or T-Mobile, or Starbucks, or Tableau, or Zillow, or Alaska Air, or REI, or . . . you get it; there are a lot of corporations here in Seattle. I now could not imagine trying to establish myself at another corporation, starting another slog up the ladder. I had made it to vice president. I was thinking I could apply for VP or SVP jobs or the equivalent of such and get paid pretty damn well in this city, but I was hearing another calling. I wanted to create. I wanted to *make* something.

At corporations, there are way too many people who don't actually make anything, so they're entirely focused on politics. I couldn't fathom any job satisfaction in a corporate, political environment. I had been incredibly lucky at Microsoft to have the air cover to avoid most of the politics and to work in a job where I could produce a ton of tangible work that literally everybody could see.

What I really wanted to do was what I was doing during that short golden period at Windows where it seemed like we were about to disrupt the status quo and implement a new model.

I also started thinking about how Redfin and companies like that really don't need ad agencies to make ads. Especially if they're doing one-offs. I started wondering how many mid- to large-size companies there were like Redfin that didn't work with an agency—or, if they did, didn't like it. Then I started to think of all the business units within corporations that don't work with agencies but still need to make broadcast-quality advertising creative.

■ ■ ■

What if I was a consultant for companies that don't have a Jon Sneider and don't need one full time? I thought. I could consult for a marketing leader or marketing department, similar to my role at Redfin, shepherding the TV spot through. I could create almost everything, or contract out everything the ad agency would normally do to prep a campaign, and then I could hire any production shop the client wanted. So, they could still shoot with Prettybird or Hungry Man in LA and get the exact same output as working with an agency.

Hmmm. If I had a really good creative partner who could do all the concepting, I could even write the copy. What else would we need? I guess we'd want a brand planner/research person who could build decks and pitch. They might not even need to be British. (That's a very inside-baseball joke, credit to you if you got it.) We'd want a measurement/metrics person with media-buying experience.

I bet I could replace almost every key deliverable an agency provides with five or six people. Not only that, I bet I could do it all *faster* and it would be *better*. And it would definitely be more *fun*. And our clients wouldn't need to keep us on retainer or anything. That would be part of the pitch! If you were the type of company that was trying your first campaign or only created campaigns once or twice a year, you could hire us. We'd create all the agency deliverables, hire a like-minded production shop, create your campaign, traffic it to broadcast channels, and then tell you how it did. If you liked the experience, you could hire us again and tell your friends. If you didn't, no sweat. Low commitment for any client. It would be a way for a company to make a much smaller bet on a campaign but get a much bigger return.

I wonder how many companies there are like Redfin that don't really need an ad agency and would love this type of service? I wonder if I could work my way into individual business groups within corporations like this?

Give Me a Month or So

The more I thought about this idea, the more I liked it. I wrote the first pitch deck in about twenty minutes.

I sent it around to a few people to start to pressure-test the idea. It seemed so simple, but I also didn't see anyone else doing it. People I sent the deck to liked the concept and thought it was legit. A lot of these people were heavy hitters in the industry.

I asked them, "Would you take a meeting with someone who came in with this pitch?"

"Yes."

"Okay. Give me a month or so."

I registered the Wild Gravity URL, ordered business cards, polished up the deck, and announced the business on Facebook. I described the vision and asked if anyone wanted to work on it with me. Here's the deck and that post.

I had about ten highly talented people with significant industry experience respond that they were super interested in helping to build Wild Gravity. There was no discussion of pay or anything like that. We just started working on it.

There was a woman who had worked in the central marketing

group at Microsoft when I was running ads for Windows. She was in charge of metrics for all of our advertising. She had once come in with a presentation showing all the best practices for television commercials. For example: say the brand name in the first five seconds, repeat the brand name X number of times, have an actionable offer, close with a call-to-action, and repeat the brand and product name at the end. Basic but highly impactful tactics.

I asked her if she wanted to be my co-founder. I told her, "You're gonna be our secret weapon. We're going to go into boardrooms and say we've deconstructed the creative process; here's the formula. We can reconstruct it for your brand. We know this works. Here's the data. We can have one of these spots ready for you in a few weeks." She was into it.

She started working on our initial business documents and partnership papers. I had one guy here in the Seattle area, Jonathan Harris, who I had intersected with at Microsoft, where he was the creative director for the Windows brand team. He had worked for my friend and colleague, and we had always gotten along. I had even been on his interview loop and yes, I gave him a "hire."

We met in person and beyond hit it off. We would be talking about the vision and were so on the same page, I was always saying things like, "You're in my head, dude!" Jonathan was on board with the vision and was psyched to help me build Wild Gravity. He had the creative chops and the marketing chops, and we already knew we got along.

The larger group was all remote, so we would meet biweekly on conference calls. Since Jonathan and I both lived in the Seattle area, we got into a habit of meeting in person at a co-working space with a whiteboard and conferencing-in the rest of the group from there. The two of us would work together before and after the call. We, as a group, started working on our website, making a professional-looking pitch deck and refining our positioning.

On Fire

The more work we did on it, the more people kind of weeded themselves out. I describe it like that scene in *Forrest Gump* when he was running, except somewhat in reverse. I started running and suddenly there were ten people running next to me, but then people started falling off. I was down to eight, then six. It held steady there for a bit and certain people started to appear stronger than others.

People were distributed around the country; the woman I had originally courted to be my founding partner lived in Illinois. The more we worked on the vision of our company, the more apparent it became that she didn't want to be part of the business development process. This did *not* fly with me. I wanted everyone to be involved with business development, especially her.

At the beginning, I did have some pretty *wild* ideas about how the business could be structured. One idea I had was that the business would have no employees. Every person who worked for Wild Gravity would be a contractor. It was an interesting thought that we poked at for a bit. Under this concept, whoever brought in a piece of business would get a commission on it, and then we would all work on it as contractors. In my vision, *anyone* could bring us a project and earn a commission.

One of the things I wanted to avoid in our model was having to expand and contract with layoffs like my previous shop had to do. I had been thinking that a majority of the workforce would be freelance and contract employees, so while we were concepting the model I said, "What if nobody worked there, literally? We have no office and no employees, including ourselves. Wild Gravity would be an entity that could hire us for jobs and pay bills and everything else a company does, but if we had no employees, we would never have to have layoffs!"

Everyone thought that was a little too much. So we thought, *What if it's a hybrid workforce with a core team of pros that expands with contractors when necessary?* That sounded pretty good.

Every single thing about Wild Gravity was supposed to be as lean and efficient as possible. We threw around the old Nissan Xterra tagline, "Everything you need, nothing you don't."

On top of this, everyone would be hyperfocused on biz dev. I'm fond of saying, "There's no biz without biz dev." I said whoever brought in the client would get 5 percent of the fee as commission; 5 percent of gross. Even me. I wouldn't get any more or less than anyone else. A lot of head nods to all of this.

Jonathan and I continued to hit it off when we were working together. At the time, we were trying to land on the logo and finish the website. I've led about a zillion digital projects; that was my entire background before L.L.Bean. I know how to lead any creative project. But somehow, I was having trouble getting our small group to align on the logo for my own company. One person in particular didn't seem to like anything, but also couldn't articulate exactly what they didn't like about it or suggest ways to improve on it.

The situation was frustrating enough that Jonathan and I began cycling on the logo on our own. We finally got to a point where we said, "This is it." We still had that one dissenter who seemed to be against things and not *for* anything, so we had to move on because everyone else loved it.

Jonathan had facilitated brand-discovery sessions at Microsoft for sub-brands of the mothership, so he led the two of us through the eye-opening process for Wild Gravity.

I had invented the brand in my head, and there were things that I didn't know about it that emerged once we got down to documenting it. The two of us defined what our brand and the company would be all about, in strange little conference rooms with whiteboards. It was cool.

We realized the brand-discovery process itself was something else we could productize. Branding agencies do this type of thing—lead a brand through a discovery process in two- to four-day off-sites and then create a beautiful, insightful brand-positioning deck. Jonathan and I had both been through these types of procedures and, as mentioned, they would take days of input from the client and then weeks for the agency to build the presentation. We had done it for ourselves in about four hours.

We figured we could do this in one-day sessions and then deliver a beautiful deck summarizing anyone's brand two days later. Branding agencies charge hundreds of thousands of dollars for this. We could charge less than a quarter of what a branding agency would charge and still have a great profit margin. In addition, it would be a low-cost way for people to get to know us, see our work, and kind of take us for a test-drive.

He and I were on fire.

I was thinking, *I think I might've committed to the wrong person as founding partner.*

Dissolving Partnerships

After a few months of working on the concept, we decided it was time for everyone to meet face-to-face. We set up an off-site in the Chicago suburbs. It was five of us including me. We stayed at a Comfort Inn, and I got a suite so we would have a place to whiteboard. We bought a cheap easel and one of those giant Post-it pads.

Jonathan couldn't make that trip, but there was some reason it was important for us to move forward with it anyway. We made a lot of progress, but while we weren't all together, my original "partner" was trying to get me to sign papers making the two of us equal partners. I told her that was absurd. She didn't want to do business development and expected half the equity for doing measurement and billing.

I made it through the weekend, but I had to "dissolve the

partnership" with her when I got back. That's another story for another book, but fortunately I was able to dissolve the Illinois connection without involving lawyers. So now we were down to four people: me, Jonathan, the dissenter in Boston, and our digital guy in Portland, Oregon, who was building the website.

I had known the guy in Boston for a long time and we'd always had great conversations about marketing and business in general in the past, but for some reason we seemed to be butting heads on items for Wild Gravity. A lot.

He was supposed to be in charge of copy, but no one was liking what he was writing. I tried to cycle with him directly. Not my first rodeo. I know how to coach without taking over, but he kept being super resistant to suggestions. He started giving off a weird vibe, different from all the times we had hung out. Since he was taking such a long time to make copy changes, I ended up writing or rewriting all the copy. Something started to feel off. I was getting this gnawing pit in my stomach and was thinking I'd have to tell him this was not working out. But he was like family. This was going to be awkward. He called me one night and said he didn't think it was working out. I agreed.

What I would find out later was that he had been working on his own website the whole time and had plagiarized our model and copy. He didn't want to hear feedback on his copy because he was taking everything we talked about and using it for himself. This story is also for the other book, but let's just say, be careful when you're starting a business. You don't want to have your buddy sign an NDA when the whole thing is still conceptual, but you might find that "FrieNDA" is not as strong as you thought.

And then there were three.

Now our group was feeling pretty tight. We each had our specific roles: I was marketing/biz, Jonathan was creative, the two of us were campaign development, and our digital guy, well, he did digital.

We got the website up and then started pitching! Jonathan and I did. Digital dude was in Portland. People were liking our pitch. A want-to-be incubator founder wanted us to be the marketing resource for his incubator and was offering free office space in the same building as his startups. We weren't sure about him or them, but they hired us for a brand-discovery session for one of their startups and we got our first small bit of revenue, like eighteen hundred bucks. Earlier, I had opened up a corporate credit card that had about nine hundred dollars on there from startup costs like registering the business, launching the site, printing cards, and things like that. So, just like that we had cleared our debt and we were in the black. Ha.

Also at this time, we were starting to line up meetings at Microsoft and Amazon.

The Gold Mine

Remember the filmmaker who'd been renovating the old building in Seattle back when I was at Redfin? Well, it was done, and it was spectacular. Two floors of mixed office space with twenty-foot ceilings, polished hardwood floors, exposed brick walls, glassed-in offices, a speakeasy-style bar, half-court basketball, four client-facing edit suites, a giant mural from a local street artist, laundry, ten visual effects stations, and a nap room. It was a seriously incredible space for production and post-production. He offered to let me and Jonathan work out of the space for free because I had basically launched his career. We decided to co-pitch Microsoft and Amazon. Wild Gravity would be the "agency," and his new company would be the production house. We would split the fee fifty-fifty—a sweet deal for us since he was supporting a small company and there was only the three of us at Wild Gravity. No overhead at all.

The filmmaker/renovator brought up something once we started coming into the office and working on things together. Turned out he was kind of sick of the ad production game and wanted to move down to LA and make a feature film. It had always been his dream. He said, "Why don't we structure a deal so you guys can just take this over and buy me out over time? I'll give you super friendly terms." Jonathan and I were flipping-out ecstatic. Digital dude, not so much.

Having been in the industry for twenty years, I had developed a reputation as a straight shooter, someone who always delivered and who was fun to hang out with, so I have a robust network of old colleagues that had become friends. People were happy to meet for coffee, lunch, or a beer and hear our pitch. In the meetings, the feedback was, "What you're saying makes a ton of sense." We got invited into the big conference rooms at the big corporations to pitch projects. We were just waiting for the first real project to land.

Remember the woman who'd been running digital video for me at Microsoft? Well, she was now a marketing director on the Amazon Fire TV team. We met for happy hour in South Lake Union in Seattle, near Amazon headquarters. She told me they needed in-product video to teach people how to use the device and find content. I told her we would love to pitch some ideas.

A week later we met with her team in the Day 1 building at Amazon, where we were briefed on the project. The brief was to create five videos for five different scenarios, such as how to use the remote control and how to search with your voice. The videos would need to come in around ten grand a pop, but there would be some wiggle room on price for the first batch. We'd be pitching against two other shops.

We brainstormed five different creative approaches or platforms. The first platform idea was called living-room host. We were friends with the star of *The Bachelor*, Season 13, and his wife, whom he proposed to on the show (they're still married!). The idea was to film from "their living room," and they would show viewers how to use their Fire TV devices. The second concept involved stop-motion animation using cardboard cutouts created from Amazon boxes. The third was an *Anchorman*-type anchorman. The fourth was a top-down time-lapse shot of an artist sketching frames of shows that would come to life. The fifth was an all-visual-effects animated option.

All the ideas were cool. We were so genuinely confident and enthusiastic, we killed at the presentation. We unofficially got the nod at the end of the pitch. We were beyond psyched. We were going to have Amazon as our first real client!

We were thinking five videos at around $10K each, maybe up to $20K for the first batch, depending on what concept they picked. So this project was likely to come in at $50K to $100K. Not bad for our first real job.

This was our conversation on our way out of the Day 1 building at Amazon. As we were getting into the Uber I got the call:

"You guys got it! For sure. My boss loved it."

"Great, which creative platform do you guys want to go with?"

"All five."

"All five? Cool, cool. So which scenarios did you want us to do? I imagine you want us to pick one or two scenarios and then test them across the five platforms."

"No, we want to do all five scenarios, for all five platforms."

"That's twenty-five videos. I mean obviously, you can do math."

"Yeah! Congratulations!"

We were flipping out now. We were high-fiving in the car. We were hugging. The phone rang again.

"We're going to need you to localize for four other markets as well: UK, Germany, France, and Japan."

"Which of the videos do you want loc'd?"

"All of them."

"That's one hundred and twenty-five videos."

Now we got quiet. *Holy fuck.*

There were four of us in the car and only two more of us back at the shop.

We weren't quiet for long. This was now a seven-figure job. We had the SOW done by the end of the day. We staffed up from six to sixty in two days. We had two film crews and an animation crew running in parallel. Every single person on that job was a pro that had done these things hundreds of times, including us.

We finished production in about two weeks, including several shoots that had to be in-language for German, Japanese, and French, and went into post. Post and VFX ran us to about four weeks. Color, sound, finishing, and localization took us to six weeks. We delivered over one hundred finished fifteen-second videos along with hundreds of corresponding static assets, to five different markets, in six weeks. Wild Gravity was off like a rocket.

You can see some of the work we used in that pitch here.

At the end of this insane project, the owner of the production studio was ready to sell and go work on his dream of writing a feature film. We wanted in. Digital dude was not down with taking on the overhead of a location and employees. He felt like we were taking a big risk. Jonathan said to him, "It's like the three of us have been panning for gold over the last three months and this guy is up the river with a fully operational gold mine that he wants to sell us." I thought it was a great analogy. Digital dude, not so much. He wanted the three of us to keep panning for gold. Jonathan and I wanted the gold mine.

And then there were two.

We structured the Amazon deal to be able to buy out my friend. We took over the space and equipment, and we kept all the staff. So next thing you know, this glorious production studio was ours. We were a real, legit business. Just like that.

It wasn't exactly like that, at all. It was a fraught process that dragged on and strained our relationship with the former owner. However, we were able to complete the deal before that happened, and now we owned a production company.

Our model had just changed a bit too, right there. Did you catch it? We had been pitching ourselves as agency services without the agency, but now we owned a production company. Our offering evolved to: agency services, production, post, and VFX, all under one roof. The ultimate hybrid shop. We *had* it.

We pitched like crazy. We won some pitches at Microsoft right away. We inherited the advertising account at Woodland Park Zoo, which was so damn rewarding. The first year in business was all the insanity that we expected, that we wanted, and more.

In three months we went from two dudes with business cards and a slide deck with no capital, no place of business, and no employees, to owners of a multimillion-dollar creative production shop with six employees in one of the coolest spaces in Seattle.

It was an incredible time. We were really busy and we were able to build the company we always wanted to build—exactly how we wanted to build it.

And now I'll tell you how we did it and how you can too.

PART II

HACKING ADVERTISING

Make everything as simple as possible, but not simpler.

—Albert Einstein

The opportunity to design a company to your exact specifications is a rare thing indeed. After two decades in the industry, I was beyond excited to put the many ideas I had into practice. I had the time—a six-month severance package from my last job—and the resources—the ten super-smart people who initially joined me pre-launch—to thoughtfully and methodically create the Wild Gravity brand and operational structure.

It came down to a few main concepts.

The vision was to form a company that could create world-class advertising and marketing creative that would rival the work of the globe's top advertising agencies, with a fraction of the people, time, and cost of *any* advertising agency.

The premise was (and still is) that it would be possible to remove all the unnecessary processes, procedures, and teams employed by agencies and make better work, cheaper and faster.

The old adage is: Good, Fast, Cheap. Pick two. Wild Gravity would deliver on all three.

More than eight years later, I'm proud to report that we do deliver on that promise, and the ability to do so comes down to four main requisites.

The Creative Process—A maniacal focus on only those things that result in better creative is fundamental, along with a ruthless resolve to remove any and all blockers of that objective.

The Structure—An organizational structure that brings key resources in-house and fosters creative collaboration across disciplines.

The Team—An A-team of seasoned ad and production professionals with a get-shit-done mindset.

The Principles and Service—Bulletproof principles and next-level *service*.

Tactically it works like this:

- Massively simplified ad-creation process
- Creative, Production, and Post, all under one roof
- Small teams of seasoned pros
- A get-shit-done culture

That's it.

Now let's talk about how this works in practice.

Chapter 6

Hack Creative Production

At Wild Gravity we approach our jobs with the understanding that, without a doubt, the most important thing in advertising is the creative. At the end of the day, all that matters is this: *Do you have an effective creative asset that is on-brand and on-message, that drives a desired behavior from a targeted audience?* That is the client's goal, so that is our goal from the outset, and it drives every aspect of how we run the shop.

Have a Bias for Making Stuff

As our primary investment is the creative, we have a bias for making stuff. We don't want to spend weeks on strategy, talking about what we *could* make. We want to make stuff and get it into market as fast as possible. At the end of the day, the only true test of a piece of creative is the market.

The goal is to make outstanding creative as efficiently as possible—that is, with the least amount of time, people, and cost possible. To do that you need to know a few shortcuts that will get you to the desired result faster than an agency would.

Organizations will be more effective by making small bets and getting more creative into market, learning and iterating along the way, than by making big, infrequent bets hedged by pre-market testing. This is a point of view. This is our stance. We don't have slides to back this up, but I know for sure that when I was the client about to make this type of change, the ROI would have been in the tens of millions of dollars if we had flipped to that type of production model.

The call-to-action on our first pitch deck was: "Skip the Bullshit. Go-to-Market."

I still love it. It's everything Wild Gravity to me. We only care about making the best piece of creative possible within the constraints that we have. Tell us the amount of time and money there is, and we will tell you the best possible creative solution that can be made within those constraints.

We promise you, there will not be twenty strategy slides before we get to the creative concepts. The work will still be *strategic*. We count on the client to know what their marketing strategy is, and then we deliver on the tactics needed to execute their strategy. We'll build a *creative strategy*, but we don't believe clients should outsource marketing strategy to agencies, and we don't presume to know the clients' strategy better than they do.

It's a huge time-saver for us. Clients never miss it. No client ever said, "I wish there had been more strategy slides in that presentation."

Marketers in charge of a big brand who run big shops should evaluate what their internal strategy team is responsible for and what the agency strategy team is responsible for. How much value is that additional strategy layer adding? How much is the agency strategy team billing you each year?

We believe that tactics writ large are more important than strategy. Strategy is crucial, of course, but the quality of the tactical execution is what drives success or failure . . . for every endeavor. Everyone who is working on the project is smart and creative—so get something into market. I'm a sucker for General George S. Patton quotes, and one of my favs is, "A good plan . . . executed now is better than a perfect plan next week."[1] Don't waste days planning when you could be spending those days learning from the in-market performance of your creative.

Obviously you want to make good bets, so one thing you want to get really good at is generating a lot of impactful concepts quickly. My partner, Jonathan, and I can develop campaign concepts for clients in a quick half-hour meeting, where it might take an agency days, if not weeks, to develop concepts. I describe the process next, where we start with established advertising *bits* and then mold them to the brief. Here's what you need to brainstorm like a pro.

---

1   Brett and Kate McKay, "General Patton's Strategy for Winning in War and Life: Keep Punching," *Art of Manliness*, updated September 25, 2021, https://www.artofmanliness.com/character/manly-lessonsgeneral-pattons-strategy-for-winning-in-war-and-life-keep-punching/.

Steal Like an Artist to Develop Great Concepts ... Fast

Pablo Picasso is credited with saying, "Good artists borrow; great artists steal."[2] I love this quote so much, because creatives tend to obsess over originality.

A lot of time is wasted in creative brainstorms because creatives, by nature, want to be original. It makes sense. They're *creative*.

The thing is, that's not what a reader or viewer wants. There are rules to narratives that are thousands of years old. All major plays, novels, movies, stories of any kind unfold according to the same general formulas.

As anyone reading this book has heard, there are only seven story archetypes, or thirty-six plot types, or whatever the number is. The point is, it's a limited number. There are not an infinite number of plots. One could write a novel or movie outside of one of these paradigms. That's possible. It would be original. But no one would like it. These story archetypes are ingrained in the human psyche.

Every movie unfolds in five acts. There's a protagonist and an antagonist. There's a love interest if it's that type of movie. There's an insurmountable conflict. It's temporarily thwarted. Comes back worse than ever. It looks like all is lost. The hero looks like he or she is dead, dying, or has given up. But then! The hero emerges from the rubble for a final victory. Cut to hero on horse or in spaceship. Sunset. And, scene.

---

2   "Quote Origin: Good Artists Copy; Great Artists Steal," *Quote Investigator*, March 6, 2013, https://quoteinvestigator.com/2013/03/06/artists-steal/.

There's a formula.

The same is true of ads. We don't have five acts, like a play, or characters who develop. But there are tried-and-true formulas generally referred to as *bits*. Examples include the taste test, everyday low prices, the before and after, the testimonial, the extended metaphor, the embarrassing mistake, the hero mom, the talking pet, talking baby, young guy dressed as old guy, and many others.

There are a lot of bits. I haven't counted them, but I like to say "there are only one hundred bits in advertising." I use the number one hundred to illustrate that there are enough bits that you might think there's an infinite number of them, but the universe of bits is in fact finite.

Once you know there are only so many bits to choose from, the question simply becomes, what bits would work great for this brief? We put the parameters of the brief on a whiteboard and start brainstorming: *What bits would work to solve this marketing problem?* It's a lot easier for a creative team to be creative when you ask what are three to five bits that would work for this brief?

It's a much quicker way. We can brainstorm three to five spots in under an hour that way. We do it all the time and it doesn't mean it's less creative. It's more creative and much more effective.

If you've ever seen Robert Altman's film *The Player*, you know what I'm talking about. Tim Robbins plays a Hollywood producer, and people pitch him movie ideas throughout the film. The way they always shortcut the pitch is to say, it's like this but it's this; it's like this hit movie combined with this other hit movie. To quote: "It's *The Graduate, Part Two* . . . It's *Out of Africa* meets *Pretty Woman* . . . It's *Ghost* meets *The Manchurian Candidate*."[3] These are all from the opening shot of the film. If you haven't seen it, you should watch it tonight. Masterpiece. With great lessons on how to pitch and create stories.

It works that way in real life too, because that's how the human brain works. Creative works that we think of as cool, are riffs on other things we think are cool. New things we like are similar to old things we like, with a twist.

For example, look at music. Rock and roll was derived from the blues, which evolved from jazz. Reggae, country, hip-hop, funk, punk, and heavy metal are all derivatives of rock and roll. Everything's a riff on something else.

For creatives to strive for *originality* not only makes the creative task more difficult and arduous, it also makes the work less effective. If a Disney movie doesn't have a happy ending, a lot of people are going to be pissed off because Disney broke the rules.

The movie *Adaptation* is all about this. The main character discusses the formula for great movies in the movie, and then the movie follows that formula. The movie is so clever, it explicitly states what the bit is while they're doing the bit, and the audience doesn't catch on until it's in motion.

---

3   "The Player: Two Pitch Scenes," YouTube, accessed October 13, 2024, 2:18, https://www.youtube.com/watch?v=06Ht6-Cw0RI&t=11s.

So if everything is derivative, don't fight it. Go with it. If your client sells soap, you might start by thinking of any soap ad you can remember at all and writing down all the bits they used. Then the creative brainstorm is just riffing off those bits. For example: *It's like the Irish Spring ad but it's this. It's like the Dove ad but it's this. Remember the old Ivory ads? It's like that but it's this.* It's a faster, more productive way to get to useful ideas. The creativity comes from the spin or the twist you add to the bit.

I laugh twice every time someone shows me the *pro-athlete-dressed-as-an-old-person* bit. First, because it's a great bit, and again because the person showing it to me doesn't ever seem to realize it's an endlessly recycled bit. The thing is, it doesn't matter. It still works. It's a great bit.

That's how we do it. We think of three to five bits, put them up on the whiteboard, then concept fresh takes on those bits that align with the client's marketing strategy.

We focus on one bit with one scenario per concept. At the end of our meetings, we take a picture of the whiteboard and have our graphic designer turn it into storyboards, one of us writes the copy, and we have five ad concepts in a pitch deck by end-of-day.

And the concepts are always well received. Why? You know the answer. Because they follow a formula that the client's brain was subconsciously expecting.

I have a rule for presenting concepts: Always present what the client is expecting first. If there are two home-run ideas and one is a base hit up the middle, exactly what they're expecting, present the expected one first. If you don't present the one they're expecting, they won't be able to hear the "wow" concept because they'll be wondering where the basic concept is. If you present the straight-take concept first, they can check that off in their heads and be open to hearing wow concepts. They'll still probably choose the base hit, straightforward, value-proposition presentation. Feature, benefit, feature, benefit, call-to-action. But at least they *heard* your pitch for the home run.

That's the concept we think of first. I mentioned soap earlier, but our niche is consumer technology. These products have complex value props. For example, Windows is not even something you usually buy directly. It's an "ingredient brand." It's an operating system that comes with the computer you buy. Normally. So it can be a complex message.

For a consumer technology product, the base hit would probably be a persona ad. Likely a slice of life. It might show how a modern technology worker, with the demands of a family they love and a job they love, is able to manage both seamlessly because of X technology in Y situations.

We've done this a few times.

We don't literally present the preceding, but that's the idea. The client is going to want to see that concept, so we show it to them right away. That way they can tick it off the list in their heads. Then, knock their socks off with the double off-the-wall and bring 'em both home to score all three runners with the home-run idea.

I may have extended that last metaphor too far, but clients won't have the head-space to hear your home-run idea if they don't see the base hit first.

A lot of agencies make the mistake of trying to present the home-run first, but if it doesn't land, the whole presentation is a letdown. Get on base with a standard bit before trying to knock it out of the park.

"Strategy Without Tactics Is the Slowest Route to Victory"

To quote Sun Tzu, another military strategist, "Strategy without tactics is the slowest route to victory. Tactics without strategy is the noise before defeat."[4] We think clients waste millions of dollars and thousands of hours when they outsource marketing strategy work to their ad agencies.

Many ad agencies spend a ton of time on strategy, which seemingly makes sense because any creative concepts should be driven by strategic objectives. Now, a solid strategy should be data

---

4   David Brim, "7 Powerful Lessons Sun Tzu Can Teach You about Strategy," *Filled to the Brim* (blog), January 8, 2013, https://davidbrim.com/sun-tzu-lessons-on-strategy/.

driven. A really smart shop would be so responsive to marketing and macroeconomic conditions that it would be driven by that data to develop strategies in real time in order to create the most compelling and timely advertising possible.

That sounds like a good pitch, right? At the beginning we thought so. "We're going to be *data driven*," we said. That copy was in the pitch deck at the beginning. But then we started talking about it. Tossing the idea back and forth.

I said, "You know, when I was the client, every time the agency presented a strategy to us, it was *wrong*."

And why was that?

Because there was always some new piece of information, some data point that we had that they didn't have, or there was something we knew that we couldn't tell them. It was always, "That strategy would make a lot of sense if you guys knew this key piece of information that you don't have access to." We had a massive strategy team at Microsoft. They were really smart. The work from the agency strategy team was redundant at best.

Many times we would sit through dozens of strategy and setup slides from an agency before they presented the creative. As a client, the whole time you're thinking, *just show me the work*. All I really wanted to see was the creative.

Another problem with outsourcing strategy to an ad agency is that there's no one direct source of truth for ad measurement. There are thousands of metrics vendors, and agency strategy teams are largely reliant on a lot of different sets of soft metrics that may or may not be important or considered credible to the client. Agencies don't have access to all the internal data the client has, nor should they, so they're additionally hamstrung by only having a partial view of what their clients are seeing.

As the client I'd think, *Why do we need another agency to tell us what our marketing strategy should be when that was our job, and we were better at it?* I would rather have creative agencies focusing on tactics—that is, impactful creative—than trying to outguess our internal strategy team.

After all that reflection we thought, *You know what? Let's not do strategy. Let's take "data driven" out of our copy.*

So we did, and now we have a pretty aggressive stance on this. I think it's the client's job to be data driven, for one simple reason: The agency will never have all the data. Ever. When I was client-side, we never gave the agency all the information. The agency shouldn't have all the information. It wouldn't even be possible or feasible. What data feeds would be the source? Ratings data? Brand metrics?

Digital advertising is a different story, and for a direct response campaign, optimization based on real-time data is possible. If you're a search engine marketing firm, you'd better be data driven. In that case, the firm does have a direct data feed and can respond in real time. That's not possible in broadcast advertising, so I think it's a fallacy when traditional ad agencies claim to be data-driven strategy experts. Agencies never have the full picture of their clients' view.

Marketing strategy is the wrong thing for ad agencies to focus on. Creative strategies for spots and campaigns, yes. But the all-up marketing strategy is best handled by the client's internal strategy team. That arrangement allows each organization (client and agency) to focus on what they're best at. Keeping strategy in-house is a big time and budget saver for the client.

Even though we made a strategic choice not to include "Strategy" as one of our offerings, our work is still strategic. Our creative is always on-strategy; we just don't have the gall to pretend we know the client's business or industry better than they do. Some agencies make it their mission to do so. We do not. We make stuff. Tactical creative stuff. We think clients know what their strategy is better than we ever will, so we focus on our core competency of delivering great creative aligned to *their* strategy.

We are driven by whatever data the client chooses to share with us, and we're good with that.

Tactics are almost always more important than strategy. Here's our old friend, General George S. Patton, again: "Good tactics can save even the worst strategy. Bad tactics will destroy even the best strategy."[5]

Long story short: We don't "do strategy." Call us when you're ready to make stuff.

---

5 "Quotes," General Patton.com, accessed October 12, 2024, http://generalpatton.com/index.php/quotes/.

Chapter 7

Hack Your Organization

E very marketer worth their salt has had the same hallway conversation. Couldn't we do this easier with fewer people? The answer is yes, you could. We do it every day. And not only is it possible, but a small, talented team of seasoned professionals with discrete job functions is going to outperform a large, hierarchical team with overlapping functions every time. Here's why.

Organize for Creative Efficiency

The first reason small teams tend to outperform large teams is communication. A hierarchy necessitates a game of telephone, with message approval at every level of the chain. When I was the client at Windows and we had a mandatory change that needed to be made to the creative, I would email or call the agency and give the direction to the account manager. They would tell me, "Well, we'll run it up the chain." *What?* "We'll run it up the chain."

Here's what they meant by that. The account manager would tell the account supervisor that the client has requested a change. They would then decide if the change was in scope or not. If they decided the change was in scope, they sent the change request over to the project manager, who would ask the associate creative director if they could make the change. The ACD would then ask the designer to make the change, then report back to the account team that the change was in progress and when it would be ready, and then the account team would tell me. *Unless.*

Unless the account team decided the change was out of scope, or the creative team decided that the change shouldn't be made for some *creative* reason and they pushed back on the request. Then it went back to the client, maybe a day later, explaining the pushback against the change request. Then I would have to talk to my boss, who was hard to get time with and didn't take no for an answer, about the agency saying they didn't want to make the change.

Suffice it to say, in my exhaustive experience, hierarchy does not help with communication flow.

Small Teams of Seasoned Pros

Efficiency flows when everyone has discrete job functions—for example, producer, writer, designer, director, editor, and visual effects artist. There's little confusion about roles and responsibilities on a team like that. At every corporation and agency I've ever worked at, there are always huge issues surrounding who does what. The number of roles and responsibilities meetings I've been in, and the number of RACI/OARPI (responsibility assignment matrix) charts I've helped construct, would destroy the soul of a lesser man. That doesn't happen on small, flat teams. It's highly unlikely that the VFX artist is going to think it's their job to direct the actors.

If you were to look at our org chart, it would look more like a molecule than a pyramid, and I kind of love that. Molecules are dynamic and constantly shifting, while pyramids are heavy, solid, and hard to move or rebuild.

When there is no hierarchy, there is little bureaucracy—processes that exist for processes' sake, as part of organizational memory or as a way for one group to control other groups. The processes that exist within small teams exist because they matter to the quality of the work and the efficiency of getting it completed.

In large hierarchies, people often ask teammates, "Why do we have to do it this way?" The answer that reveals a full bureaucratic infection is when someone says, "Because we've always done it that way." It has literally become a zombie process that lives on despite nobody on the team being able to discern or define the value. Small teams don't have time for that shit.

Without hierarchy and bureaucracy, small teams move fast. Small teams moving fast and creating great work develop comradery, unlocking an even deeper level of efficiency and creativity.

Small teams have a greater sense of *we're all in this together.* Hierarchical teams tend to get parochial within their silos of creative, account, media, and other functions. When a sense of comradery develops on a team that is clicking and you're all rowing in the same direction, the work becomes fun.

When the team is in the zone, having fun and working to deliver something they *love,* that type of energy shines through. Clients can feel it, see it. That's when you get the "exceeds expectations" type of feedback, and comments like "I love working with Wild Gravity."

Can this type of energy happen in an agency? Yes. Can it be sustained? It's very difficult to keep agency teams together for an extended period of time. Every agency person will attest they've been part of great teams. Most will cite this as a specific time period, on a specific account. It is not the norm in a hierarchical org. It's the exception.

Small teams of professionals will always outperform large hierarchical teams. Always.

How to Scale Up . . . and Down at Lightning Speed

The cynical reader finished that section and thought, *Sounds great, dude, but what if you have a big client with big jobs?* As of this writing, there are five companies with trillion-dollar market caps. Two of them are our clients. This is how we handle multi-trillion-dollar clients with our ten-person shop.

The key to servicing big clients and big jobs with small teams is having separate dedicated teams for each job. We set up separate custom teams for each client job—an elite squad of industry pros. The great thing about this from a client perspective is that they always get exactly what they need and nothing or nobody that they don't need. Since each team is custom built and we don't have anyone sitting on the bench who needs hours, we never miss-staff anyone. We don't have extra people. There are no junior staff members looking for a learning opportunity. You'll never come into our offices and have someone say, "We're going to have the junior creatives present to you this time," because we don't have any junior creatives on the bench. Each client gets their own team of elite industry professionals with eras of experience.

This is also how we can scale in an instant. And *scale down* when the job is over, without layoffs. We expand and contract with freelancers and contract employees. We have a core group at our shop of between ten and fifteen people. We can make anything from a TikTok to a feature film with just our team. We've done it. But when there's more than one big job, we need to make mirror versions of ourselves, and we do. We don't hire them as full-time employees, though.

The great thing about the production industry is that it's already set up that way. Most people are freelance; they contract and work gig to gig. It's generally always easy to quickly staff up for a new job. It's easy for us because it's part of our strategy, so we do three things consciously.

First, we give our freelancers a great place to work. Our space is amazing. It's a cool place to come and work for a few days or a few weeks, and we have room for everyone. With almost nine thousand square feet, edit/visual effects stations, client-facing edit suites, and state-of-the art conference room and work-spaces, we have the room to fit everybody, and it's a space where people want to come to work.

Second, we treat people well. Buy everybody lunch. Provide parking. And we're nice and create a fun environment. Sounds simple, but lots of shops don't do this.

Third, we *pay them*. We pay everyone fairly. We pay them on time. We don't dick around on the most important part of it. Everyone appreciates that. Shops that don't pay their vendors on time won't have their choice of vendors on the next gig.

Because of this, we have a great rep and we can always scale up in an instant. The freelance community is always eager to work with us.

That strategy has served us well. Hybrid shop owners often think, *If we're setting up a shop with everything under one roof, everyone has to be a full-time employee.* And it's not an unreasonable assumption. If you're going to say you do everything in-house, it means everyone works for you, right? I saw two shops try it this way.

The content marketing shop tried it that way. They grew fast but then also had to contract when they lost their big account. Same thing with the shop we bought out. I saw both these guys grow from about ten to more than thirty people and then go through layoffs and then hire up again and then go through layoffs.

Even in LA, you can only go through that cycle a few times before you burn out the workforce and gain a reputation as a place to stay away from. I had it in my mind that I did not want to do that. I thought, *You can still keep everything in-house, even if you're staffing jobs with contract employees rather than FTEs.*

Because we scale with freelancers, when the gig is over it's all high-fives and "see you next time," rather than pink slips and tears.

Freelancers can be expensive. They cost about twice as much per hour, in general, than someone on salary. For that reason, if someone really stands out as a freelancer and the work seems like it's going to be steady for that capability, we'll bring them on full time. If they want to. Many freelancers don't want a full-time gig, so it's a dance.

One lesson we learned the hard way was not to go through this process too fast. Culture is precious at a small company, and one or two people with negative energy can turn the atmosphere for a dozen other people.

Recently, we got a brief from Microsoft to create eight case-study videos for a conference in *one month*. Half of our shop mobilized to Europe to shoot at LEGO in Denmark, Carl Zeiss in Germany, and Domino's Pizza in the UK. The footage looks cinematic, the clients loved the work, and they reported we were the only vendor that delivered flawlessly, on time, and on budget. I can assure you this model works.

The Formula for Success:
The Five Magic Metrics©

As an advertising professional you will be bombarded with advertising metrics. There are literally thousands of different ad metrics you could focus on, but there are just five that you must nail to ensure the success of your commercial (or any piece of marketing creative). I call these five metrics the Five Magic Metrics because when you hit on all five, magic happens.

Between L.L.Bean, Windows, and Redfin, I have executed over $1 billion in media buys and run thousands of commercials. When creating a television commercial, you must be crystal clear on your tactical objectives—specifically, what metrics are you trying to drive.

These metrics are Breakthrough, Brand/Product Recall, Message Recall, Likeability, and Purchase Intent. These metrics form a cascading funnel, meaning if you don't score high in the first metric, your score is limited in the next.

For example, if you don't score high in Breakthrough, then you can't score high in Brand Recall. If you don't score high in Breakthrough and Brand Recall, then you're not going to score high in Message Recall.

And so on.

Here's how the metrics work:

1. Breakthrough: Did you remember seeing the ad?

2. Brand/Product Recall: Do you remember what the ad was for?

3. Message Recall: Do you remember the main message from the ad?

4. Likeability: Did you like it?

5. Purchase Intent: Would you buy this product?

Let's see how this works in a particular industry. I like to use the insurance industry as an example because insurance companies spend a tremendous amount of money on advertising. The industry is rife with well-known brands competing for attention in order to differentiate a product that is essentially a commodity.

Far and away, the best television advertiser in the industry is GEICO. They hit on all five of the magic metrics with every campaign. Let me show you how.

Here's a mock survey to measure advertising effectiveness.

- Do you remember seeing an ad last night with a caveman, a gecko, or a camel talking about hump day?

- What was it for?

- What was the message?
- Did you like it?
- Would you consider purchasing this product/service?

GEICO scores super high in Breakthrough. Everyone remembers the ads with the Caveman, the Gecko, and the Camel. People know they're from GEICO—high Product Recall. *And* everyone recalls the message: save 15 percent or more for your insurance. Are they Likable? People love those ads. Because they score high on the first four metrics, a lot of us have called the 800 number or checked the website to see if we qualify—Purchase Intent.

GEICO scores high on every metric, and it all cascades from great Breakthrough. I believe GEICO is the best advertiser in that industry, and they are likely the most successful television advertiser overall for the last ten years or longer.

Now let's compare GEICO to Liberty Mutual.

- Do you remember seeing an ad with a character named Doug and an emu?

Far fewer people remember Doug and Emu from Liberty Mutual's campaigns, so they don't score as high on Breakthrough. Because of that, even fewer people connect those characters to Liberty Mutual, equaling lower Brand Recall. Their message is "only pay for what you need," which is neither memorable nor compelling, so we would expect to see low Message Recall. Their ads seem likeable enough, but that score is severely limited because they don't break through or drive recall. Is Purchase

Intent high for Liberty Mutual? I have no access to their internal metrics, but I can tell you for sure that those ads don't drive significant Purchase Intent.

I won't go through every insurance advertiser, but now you have a framework to judge the likely effectiveness of any advertising or marketing creative asset. You can apply that framework to evaluate any ad and understand through observation what is successful and what is not. You have the tools to consider whether Jake from State Farm is effective or not.

Most important, now that you understand the Five Magic Metrics, you understand how to create impactful advertising and marketing creative for your brand.

Nail these metrics and let the magic happen!

Chapter 8

Hack Client Service

At the beginning of my advertising career, working as an account supervisor at Digitas, Boston, I was flying to Detroit every other week and spending two days and a night in the RenCen (Renaissance Center—GM headquarters), presenting all the super-smart ways we were spending our client's many millions of dollars in a channel they didn't understand. In my early agency days, I had the opportunity to lead accounts for AT&T, Microsoft, and Turner networks. I went client-side at Fidelity, where I was brought on to lead the redesign of fidelity.com. From there, I was head of advertising at L.L.Bean; director of advertising, online advertising, and social media for Windows; and vice president of advertising and brand at Redfin.

My business partner, cofounder, and executive creative director of Wild Gravity, Jonathan Harris, drove the creative in all the hot agencies in Seattle, on all the big brands in town, and then as global creative director for Windows at Microsoft. He knows what assets are going to be needed in the H2 BOM (Microsoft jargon for bill of materials for the second half of their fiscal year). He's built scores of brand libraries. He's led brand shoots all over the world. He's interviewed C-level executives from giant brands and corporations. He's led creative projects for brands like LEGO, HBO, the NBA, Amazon, Accenture, and many more.

Combined, the two of us have worked with and delivered for a significant number of *giant-ass brands*. We have walked the halls, presented in, created work for, and helped generate business for scores of corporations.

Tell Them What They *Really* Need

Why does any of this matter? We are fluent in corporate-speak. We get jargon. We know a shit-ton of acronyms. We know how to navigate complicated corporate bureaucracies. We know our clients are going to need things like brand and engineering approval and who they need to contact to get that approval. We understand what clients really need, often before they do. We were the clients. We cut to the chase. I mean, that's our job, but sometimes it seems like a magic trick to our clients, when they come in and ask for something vague or don't know exactly what they need, and we say, "What you *really* need is this." *Fairy dust and reveal.* And they agree.

Here's a quick example of how this works in practice. When Microsoft was prepping for the most recent Windows launch, the Windows business-to-business team came to Wild Gravity and said, "The consumer marketing team is making a video for launch, and we want you guys to make a version of that, showing business scenarios. Where possible, we want you to take the existing video, re-cut it, take out the screens that show consumer scenarios, and put in new screens that show business scenarios."

It wasn't the best brief, but we always show the client what they asked for first before presenting other options. They sent us the list of seven scenarios. A week later they called and said, "Bad news, the video that the consumer video team created was killed in an executive review. There's nothing to edit, rip, and replace."

We said, "Why don't we just shoot a new launch video?"

They said, "There's no time for that. There's less than three weeks before launch."

We said, "We don't think that's a problem. We'll start casting today, we can shoot here, build and animate all the screens, comp, rotoscope, VFX, color, and finish, all right here. We think we can pull it off."

We had it cast in two days. We were shooting at our studio by the end of the week. Our team worked directly with Windows engineers, designers, and the brand team to build screens and screen animations that were pixel perfect.

The video was so well received by Windows executives, it was featured in the chief product officer's keynote speech at launch and was the main asset on the center well of Windows.com.

We truly believe there's only one shop that could have pulled that off. We built the model, have the resources, *and* we've got the street smarts. We can cast it, shoot it, edit it, build and animate screens, host all the reviews, create all the locs, export all the versions, and do it all within our four walls with our crew. But our real superpower is the ability to thin slice to the exact creative asset that's needed, often faster than our clients.

In this case we said, "Look, you have seven scenarios. We'll shoot something loosely story-based that works together as a single piece, but it'll also be modular so we can make cutdowns to market each individual scenario. You'll get one main video and seven cutdowns to run on social media."

It's safe to say Jonathan and I have our ten thousand hours. Our whole shop has been to the rodeo so many times we can map out the concession stands and bathrooms, and make sure our client doesn't ride the angry bull.

We want to make sure our clients look like heroes and deliver a prized asset when it looked like all hope was lost.

Faster Than a Speeding Client

A consistent client-ask is, "How fast can you make it?"

This is such a loaded question, and the answer is one that needs to be finessed. The answer we used to give is: "We can move as fast as you can."

Basically, we're telling the client that we move much faster than they do and that most likely, client delays will be the limiting factor on any given production.

Production experts will tell you that any creative project is limited by the speed of the client's internal processes. Universally, delays in production timelines are caused by three things: delay getting the PO opened, delayed delivery of brand assets, and slow review/approval turnaround times.

All the things that can add time or delay a project are typically on the client side. It's a delicate message to deliver. But if the client can get the PO open right away, supply all the assets at kickoff, and turn approvals around in hours . . . well, then, is the end of next week fast enough?

The simple answer is that if we have all those things lined up, we can hit almost any date. We could deliver creative in under twenty-four hours if all the right resources and infrastructure was in place. My old shop did it with Bud Light. That's not the point.

The point is that our speed is almost never the limiting factor.

When it comes to the things we can control, we do them all as fast as they can possibly be done while maintaining top-tier quality. How do we do this? We move fast but we never rush. Because we all have our ten thousand hours, we can thin slice a lot and we're not shy about it. We trust our expertise.

We are not anti-process. We are anti processes that don't lead to making *better creative faster*. Our brainstorming process is a good example; we don't need to start with the whole universe of ideas. We're all experts. Let's quickly think of three to five creative devices that would work and then let's *make* them work.

To this end, the tool kit of assets is one solution that always stays fresh. If a client has a dozen or more different markets with varied tiers of budget, we know they're going to need a "tool kit" with three tiers of assets. The highest-production-value assets will go to the tier-one markets. Less expensive localized versions will go to the tier-two markets. Tier-three markets will get a DIY kit they can use to make their own assets.

I was talking to my old boss at the content marketing agency, and I said to him, "It's always the same problem."

He replied, "I know. Let's never tell them."

I thought that was borderline not-the-right-thing-to-do when he first said it, but then I tried being transparent in a couple of client meetings, saying, "Well I've heard this problem before and—"

I'd always get cut off with, "No, no, no, our situation is totally unique," and then they'd follow up with, "We have three tiers of markets that need different levels of creative assets." Then I'd say, "You're right, that *is* unique. What if we made a tool kit where your tier-one markets get the highest-production-value assets, tier two gets a less expensive version, and tier-three markets get a DIY kit?"

"Oh a tool kit! Brilliant."

The point here is we're not shy about using our expertise to get to an answer more quickly, even if it subverts a standard, accepted process. Our deep industry experience allows us to thin slice and jump straight to the answer—to get the client what they *really* need (even when they didn't know what it was).

Throw Down the Cocktail Napkin

I was a bartender. There are two types of bartenders.

One type of bartender keeps their head down when they get busy. They knock out order after order, but they never look up and make eye contact. If you're waiting at the bar, it stresses you out because you don't know if the bartender has seen you or not, or when you'll get to order.

The other type of bartender does the exact same amount of work, but they keep their head up, and when someone new walks up to the bar they throw down a cocktail napkin, make eye contact, and say, "I'm really busy, but I'll be right with you."

It takes the same amount of time for each bartender to serve drinks. The drinks taste exactly the same. But one experience was much better than the other. So, what's the difference?

The *communication*. The second bartender clearly communicated, "I *see* you. I'm busy. This is what I'm doing. You're next." Recognition, status update, and expectation setting. It doesn't take a lot of time. It actually takes no extra time.

At Wild Gravity, we always preach, "Be the bartender who throws down the cocktail napkin." How does this translate to making ads? We're not serving drinks, true. But the principle is the same.

If a client emails with a question or a change request that will take some time to answer, many people will wait until they have the answer to respond. What we do, instead, is respond immediately, saying something to the effect of, "I see your email. I don't have the answer yet, but I'm hunting it down. I should have it by end of day." Recognition, status update, and expectation setting.

The difference between doing that versus not responding until we have the answer is the difference between a client who is stressed out all day, not knowing if the request was heard, and a client who is free to focus on other things, knowing their request is being taken care of.

Even though we deliver a product to our clients, we are essentially a service business. Our clients have many options when it comes to who to work with. The experience is just as important as the end deliverable to them.

Since we've been there, we know that one bad soundbite going around the client's office can kill your engagement there. All it takes is for one person to say, "Well, they were kind of hard to work with" for your business to suddenly dry up.

It's not only important to do a great job but also to constantly communicate exactly what you're doing. Never assume the client knows what you're doing for them. *If you don't tell them, they don't know.*

If you have a service business for the largest brands in the world, it's not good enough for people to like working with you; they have to *love* working with you, and it's these details that turn like into love.

To provide great service, throw down the cocktail napkin, make eye contact, and communicate.

Chapter 9

Hack Your Culture

I tell people all the time: I'll give you our secret sauce because it doesn't matter if you're a venture-backed MBA straight outta Stanford, you can't just copy our model. I mean, I'm giving all the secrets away right here. Here's the book. Any entrepreneur is welcome to, and should, take this book and start their own version of our shop. I sincerely want people to do that.

The reason we're so confident that nobody is going to eat our lunch is that at its core our model comes down to one thing: experience.

Everyone is a senior employee. There are no junior employees. We don't have an internship program. We have *young people*. But we don't have anyone without deep and significant experience.

Experienced People Who Get Shit Done

If you want small teams of professionals to hack the process in order to make world-class work at a fraction of the time and footprint of a traditional shop, everyone on that team has to have deep experience. Everyone on the team has to be excellent at their job and have a track record of delivering over and over again.

That's the key. If there's a criticism of our shop, I suppose it would be that we have no training program. We don't have that luxury. Everybody we hire is already an expert at their job.

American culture likes to celebrate entrepreneurs. However, they're almost always presented as "overnight successes," though this is almost never the case. Seldom is the deep experience of the entrepreneur the story, when this is perhaps the most critical factor for a startup's success.

I hold an MBA in entrepreneurship from the perennially number-one ranked business school for entrepreneurship, the F.W. Olin Graduate School of Business at Babson College. One message was drilled into us at that school: The most critical factor to the success of any startup is the experience of the founders; deep industry experience does more to ensure the success of any new business than any other factor. That is not the message you tend to hear in entrepreneurship articles, books, or conferences.

Jonathan and I pitched a talk to one of the conferences here in Seattle. We told them about how people could build hybrid shops with small teams of pros. We got to the part about how everybody has to have a lot of experience, and they were like, "Wait, people aren't going to want to hear that."

Excuse me, what?

"People don't want to hear that. They want to be the next Zuckerberg. Especially if they're hacking something, they want it to be fast."

We said, "Well, we know it's a little bit of an *eat your vegetables* message, but it's true. First of all, Zuckerberg damn straight had his *ten thousand hours*. That guy was a coding machine. He was building, rebuilding, building, rebuilding. He had a shit-ton of experience. Second, hackers are experts. You learn to hack something when you know the system so well you can create shortcuts to your benefit."

I think they were looking at it the wrong way. It shouldn't be bad news to young people that it's important to gain experience before starting a company. It should be reassuring to anyone with a job and good news to young people who are working that by excelling in your career, you are preparing yourself to one day start your own business.

The best thing you can do if you want to start a company is to first get a job in the industry you want to be in. Try to work as many jobs in the industry as you can. Find out what works and what doesn't.

That's what I did. I had nearly two decades of experience in the ad industry before launching Wild Gravity. I learned what worked and what didn't, and I found a niche in the industry that we could fill. At Wild Gravity we leverage all of our experience in order to focus solely on the activities that are going to produce the best possible piece of creative, in the most efficient way possible.

One Hundred Percent Get-Shit-Done People

Experience isn't the only quality that makes somebody a pro, and to work at Wild Gravity we have a specific type of person we look for with particular qualities.

We look for "get-shit-done people."

What are get-shit-done people? I think it's fairly obvious: They get shit done. But I think they're a lot more rare in the workforce than most people would assume. I would estimate about one in twenty, or 5 percent of people in corporations, are GSD people.

You know who these people are in your company. They're the ones who actually deliver the creative assets. They're the ones who make the stuff. They're probably you if you're reading this book. The rest are managing people and processes, going to meetings, building decks, and presenting status updates on the work other people are doing.

I do the following bit at the office. Picture two people having a conversation in the hallway at any given corporation:

- There's a ball on the ground.

- There *is* a ball on the ground.

- The ball is red.

- It is red.

- It is definitely someone's job to pick up the ball.

- It sure is.

- What should we do?

- Let's call a meeting to figure out whose job it is to pick up that ball.

- Great idea.

- Who should be there?

- Let's call a meeting to discuss who should be in the meeting.

- Sounds great. That was a lot of work. Want to get lunch?

Most people in a corporation are like that. By my estimation there's only around 5 percent of people who will see the ball on the ground and just pick it up and start moving it down the field. The people that always pick up the ball and don't worry about whose job it is are get-shit-done people—GSD peeps.

These people never let the team down. Not just because they

work hard, but because they care. They care about the work, and they care about each other.

That's the ineffable quality we look for when we ask people to work with us.

That's the quality we need everyone on our team to have, to enable us to always overdeliver. For our small team to be able to deliver world-class creative, better and faster than shops ten times our size, 100 percent of our team needs to be get-shit-done people.

Do the Right Thing

Always do the right thing, and you'll never do the wrong thing. It's not just a nice thing to do—it's a smart business decision, and it's one of the keys to Wild Gravity's success. When we started our shop there were tons of questions for my business partner and me about how to set up the company, whether about employee compensation, production, insurance budget, transparency, or any judgment calls. We would always ask "what's the right thing to do?" and we would do that.

And we're not Polly Purebred looking for kudos on our generosity and benevolence. Doing the right thing was and is a business decision. It's an investment in our employees, our clients, and all the other stakeholders. Like any good investment, doing the right things has compounding benefits.

There's a reason our employee and client retention rates are so high, and doing the right thing is the foundation of it all.

That's the reason "Do The Right Thing" is the first item on our list of values.

WILDGRAVITY.

WE

Do The Right Thing

Always Pick Up The Ball

Get Sh!t Done

Care About Each Other

Never Let The Team Down

Always Overdeliver

Can Always Do The Job

Solve Problems No One Else Can Solve

Deliver Creative No One Else Can Deliver

Throw Down The Cocktail Napkin

Have Fun

You can download our values doc here:

A successful business to us is not "my partner and I make a lot of money." That's certainly *one* of our goals, but a successful business to us is one that supports its employees and fosters a place of community and creativity where people genuinely want to come to work and collaborate together.

A successful business to us is one where clients are excited to work with us, where they trust us implicitly and explicitly—they feel taken care of, like they're working with friends. A successful business to us is one that is active in the community and supports local arts and education organizations.

You get it. There's a lot more than money that we think about when we measure the success of our business, and the guiding principle that ensures we hit those goals is: Do the right thing.

It's often tempting to *not* do the right thing. It may be to your financial benefit to cut a corner, like maybe not get the insurance you're supposed to get for your productions. This is a real case. The company we bought out never got a required insurance product needed for productions because the old owner said "we never needed it." We were like, well that's why it's called insurance. You don't usually need it, but you're insured if you do. So when it was our decision to make, we asked, "You're supposed to have it?" *Yes.* We said, "Do the right thing and get the insurance."

When you always do the right thing by your employees, they notice, they remember. They want to be there. They want to do everything they can to make the company successful. And they stay. We've had the same core of employees since we started Wild Gravity over seven years ago.

For the first five years we had an attrition rate near zero. Many companies say they want a family feel, and we think we really have it. It can be hard to maintain, but the crucial ingredient is *everyone doing the right thing.*

For clients, when you always do the right thing, the results are obvious. They love working with you. They become your *raving fans.* You get calls from their colleagues from different parts of the company when they need work. Your shop is always the first one they call when they have a job.

Doing the right thing by the *community* just hits you right in the feels. We've created work to support the local radio station, local zoo, and local film festival. It has resulted in some good exposure for us, and we have generated a couple of clients out of those efforts. The more rewarding part is to contribute to the community in a tangible way that literally everyone can see. I mean, we make videos for them. People see our contributions. It's hard to beat that feeling and then hey, next thing you know we're friends with the local DJs, filmmakers, and *zookeepers*!

Doing the right thing has a massive ROI no matter how you look at it. It costs you nothing and means everything.

PART III

HACKING AN INDUSTRY

It's not the idea,
it's the execution.

f you're in the advertising industry on the client, agency, or production side, it's likely that you're now wondering how you would implement this type of structure in your company. I want to warn you up front that this will not be easy, and I want to assure you that it will be well worth it and that (with zero hyperbole) you will unlock millions of dollars for your company. Corporate advertisers will save tens to hundreds of millions of dollars, depending on ad budgets.

If you're the client for a big brand advertiser, skipping the agency and going straight to a creative production company sounds like an easy process and an easy sell to your organization (e.g., "We're going to save millions of dollars, months of time, and be able to test all of our creative in-market"). Sounds like a no-brainer. However, be warned that you will face many internal barriers and blockers. Many people have been making a lot of money doing it the old way, and certain internal structures and organizations exist within your corporation solely to manage all the agencies. Fiefdoms may have developed around managing and supporting all these agencies. Those fiefdoms will be threatened by any talk of dismantling the current paradigm. Tread carefully, brave marketer.

Agency owners and execs, you're no doubt feeling the pressure to add production capabilities to your agency, as creative-production companies have already started to eat your lunch. What I'm saying is not new. You probably heard the keynotes at Cannes over the past decade talking about the broken agency process. The agency business is not *in danger* of being disrupted. It's *being* disrupted in a major way. You know you need to do this, maybe you've already started, and if so, you too will know that, though necessary, it is not an easy process. The biggest hurdle here is the culture. It is not enough to add production staff. They must be assimilated into the agency, and the agency people need to become production experts. Otherwise you've still got two separate organizations within your company and you'll have just produced a microcosm of the traditional process. That's not enough. This needs to be a holistic change to your company.

Production company owners, no doubt you've thought of or are in the process of adding agency capabilities to your shop. You've noticed there are fewer agencies and fewer jobs from agencies and you're watching "content creators" eat your lunch because you never marketed yourself directly to brands before. The same general caution applies to you. Adding agency staff to a production company can completely derail your company culture, add cost, and may not directly result in more sales or revenue. I watched it happen to a friend's business. Adding agency staff eventually led them to close the doors of their production company because of the preceding reasons. When you make these changes, *culture* must be a primary focus.

Chapter 10

Hack Your Brand

Okay, brave brand advertisers and marketers, you're here, you heeded the warnings, and you're not deterred. You're still thinking, let's do this. As I said, this will not be easy. You read about some of the challenges I faced in realigning three different brand advertisers, and I just glossed the surface. Fortunately, as the pioneer that returned home shot full of arrows, I can tell you how to avoid most of the barbs.

The first thing you must do is manage your rhetoric. Even if you're the CEO or CMO of a corporation, it will be difficult to disentangle giant agency relationships. If you're a marketing director it will be that much harder. Even though it's clearly the right thing to do and it will save the company tens to hundreds of millions while upleveling ad effectiveness, there will be many holdouts.

Entire orgs, unofficial fiefdoms, and various individual jobs exist within your corporation whose main job it is to manage and support the agencies. These organizations and the people within them will feel threatened by anything that upsets the apple cart, so what you say and how you say it matters.

Do not talk about *blowing up* old norms or tearing down old infrastructure. You want to talk about streamlining, adding efficiencies, and saving money. This will be a yearslong process that must be managed thoughtfully and cannot be forced.

Though it will be a revolution, it's an easier sell as an evolution.

First, Just Skip All the Bullshit

It should be clear by now that it's possible to work without an advertising agency and still be able to create world-class, cinema-quality commercials and marketing videos. Advertising executives running big brands at their companies will now want to know: "How do I make this play out at my company?" Seasoned ad execs will likely be tired of the whole agency experience—unless they like expensive and slow.

There are a lot of options out there now. I am not the first one to think of the hybrid shop idea, so the standard agency route is not the only option. Still, it is the main paradigm by which corporate advertising gets created, and it's the main paradigm for a reason: It works!

Advertising agencies are really good at their jobs. I mean *really* good. They're some of the most talented people on the planet.

Everyone's heard the old adage, "Nobody ever got fired for hiring IBM." They might be expensive. Slow. Bureaucratic. But they're going to deliver a professional product every time with a process you can trust.

You could try another vendor that might be faster, better, cheaper, but they might mess up the report that your boss depends on each month when you switch over. Better stick with IBM.

It can be the same with your embedded agencies. Ad agencies are very good at making ads. They are extremely embedded in every corporate brand. Many corporate marketing departments are structured specifically to interface with the agency. The two entities can be deeply interconnected. Even though they're expensive, bureaucratic, and slow, you know what you're going to get from them. Switching to a new process, even if it's better, faster, and costs less is *a risk*.

Nobody's going to get fired for sticking with the current paradigm. Depending on the culture, it can take a brave marketer to even consider going direct to production and skipping the whole agency process.

You, brave marketer, might build the best slide deck in the world after reading this book, proving that your Fortune 100 company could save tens of millions of dollars every year, make better ad creative, get better results, and build up internal resources, all at the same time. You might think this will be the biggest slam-dunk right before you go in front of the executive board to present.

Get ready for a shock. Embedded culture is hard to move. A lot of your peers and superiors have invested years if not decades developing skills and habits of working this way. Not only that, they have developed relationships. When relationships get threatened, people feel threatened.

Here's the first thing: As an internal operator in a corporate culture, you need to watch your rhetoric. Nobody is *blowing up* anything. You're not firing the agency. (Not yet, anyway.) No one is *throwing out the old model*.

It's an unrealistic goal, first of all, to blow up the whole paradigm. Even if you're the CEO of a huge brand with embedded agencies and you read this and said to yourself, "Y'know what? F this, I'm blowing up all agency relationships and everyone is going direct to production." It would not be a good directive. Here's why.

Agencies do provide real value. If you're going direct-to-production, you as the client need to have an incredibly detailed understanding about what exactly the agency is doing for you. Is the agency functionally an extension of your marketing team? That's going to take a lot of work to unwind.

The first thing you want to do is an audit of everything the agency is doing for your company as part of their retainer. Now sit with your team and map out all the overlapping capabilities you have. Then note where all the overlaps are. Are there a lot of areas where the agency is doing work that internal teams could easily pick up?

That's your primary focus at first. It's a fairly boring endeavor and it shouldn't ruffle anyone's feathers. You just want to stop paying for things your company doesn't really care about or could easily handle internally. Strategy is always the big overlapping capability here. That's usually tied to measurement/metrics. I've already discussed why the agency's strategy is always just off. They don't have all the data and they never will. So why pay for them to analyze it? The important thing in this phase is to audit the data inputs they do have, that you don't. Do you want any of them to come to you directly? Do you want Nielsen ratings, Comscore metrics, and the like delivered straight to your inbox? Probably a good call to have a direct feed on those anyway, no?

I don't want anyone to think this is a bait and switch, but you might very well get to a point where you say, "We don't really want to skip the whole agency. There are a whole lot of things they do for us that we want them to continue to do." That's totally fine! But there are likely a lot of services you're paying for that don't add up to more impactful creative.

How many account people do you need? Does an AAE (assistant account executive) really spend forty hours a week working on your account? What do they do for eight hours every day when there are four account people? Do you really need an escort on set?

Please don't confuse me with an agency cost consultant. The goal is not cost-cutting per se. The goal is to make the best advertising creative you've ever produced in your life. The goal is to refocus those funds and dedicate them to generating more creative assets to put into market.

To that end, you know the people at the agency you *love* working with? Yeah, the creatives. What you're going to do is take that strategy money and invest in them. Invest in that team. Hire more creatives, make more creative. Generate more content. More assets. More video. More photography. More articles. More everything.

Most important, get that creative into market. Want to know what the best focus group is? It's the market.

Want to test something? Get it in market. You can only test like that if you have lots of creative and can iterate very quickly. Creative is what is going to make your brand stand out.

Nobody ever won a Cannes Lion for a strategy deck. My goal, our goal, is not to bring down agencies but to get us all back to doing what we love: making great creative and getting it into market.

If you're a CEO hell-bent on "blowing it all up," call me and I'll be there on the first flight. Anything less than that, just skip the agency BS you don't like and invest in the part you do like. Shape the agency to work like you think it should. Don't settle for living with it because that's how they say it needs to be done.

You could be the hero that saves your company a million dollars by removing a single process that nobody cared about anyway. It happens. All. The. Time.

The agency works for you. Why are you sitting through slides you don't care about? There's a good chance you can reshape the agency footprint to get the stuff you want and skip the stuff you don't.

As mentioned and repeated, I'm not the first one to think of this. *And.* Agencies do add value. If your brand is looking at agencies, there is a whole new breed of agencies that do skip a lot of the bullshit. Today it is possible to find small, nimble shops focused on developing top-tier creative as quickly as possible. As a matter of fact, some of the guys from Big-Huge spun off to start their own shop that skips all the bullshit of the old one, and they can deliver in a fortnight.

If you are looking for an agency, look for a shop like that. If a pitch starts with how deep the strategy and account teams are, maybe you don't need to hear the rest of that pitch. Agencies in the new production landscape should be lightweight, creative-generation machines that know how to make great ads, concept big campaigns, and manage all the production partners. That's it.

Find an agency that recognizes that and is openly hostile to the old agency paradigm. If they have great creative and a great track record of delivering it on time and at speed, that's your shop.

Make a Seamless Transition

Let's say that internal politics are a nonissue and you're ready to go direct to a hybrid creative production shop. Maybe you've been managing a huge agency and can't imagine how you would possibly get all of your campaign work out the door. This is the process I would recommend.

Start small. Do not switch to a new vendor right away. Look for a hybrid shop that has creative and production under one roof or a production company with creative services. Try some one-off projects with them.

Large brands work with multiple shops all the time. There's no reason a huge agency should be threatened by a small production house. Be transparent with your agency and with the new shop. To a point.

Clearly, you're not going to tell your agency that you're hoping to replace them with a smaller, more nimble resource, but you can tell them that you're experimenting with smaller vendors for certain projects.

The key thing to look for in a creative production shop is sophistication. Does this shop have people that can sit in a room with your CEO and present a campaign? Do you feel confident that these people will be organized enough to distribute over one hundred versions of this creative asset on launch day? Does this team understand brand systems, or is your team going to have to play brand police on all of the work?

That's the type of stuff the agency does for you that you might not even be paying attention to. The agency is a filter, so you don't see the rough draft of many details. You're still going to want that service, so make sure the shop you're working with has the sophistication and infrastructure to handle a corporate brand.

If your initial productions with the new shop go well, start ramping them up and see if the new resource can scale and continue to produce high-quality creative at speed. Can this shop handle the creation and distribution of the thousands of creative assets needed to fuel your next campaign?

If so, you're off to the races!

Bring the Best Part of the Agency Home

As tempting as it is to just rip on agencies, they do provide real value, and if you're a big brand, you're going to have to replace those capabilities.

One of the biggest benefits of working with an ad agency is they work with a lot of brands besides yours. They can have a more holistic view of the industry and the market overall. There's a good chance they've seen situations similar to yours.

This is true in ways you might not expect. When we worked with Big-Huge, they also had Domino's Pizza and Best Buy. I joined Windows right after Vista and just before the Windows 7 launch. The creative strategy could be summarized as, "You spoke, we listened." All the creative had the tone of, "We heard the negative feedback on Vista, we addressed it, and we created Windows 7 based on what you the customer told us you wanted."

During this time, I remember watching a Domino's ad where the executives were listening to focus group feedback on how bad their pizza was and then introducing new pizza recipes that addressed the negative feedback. Same strategy. *You spoke, we listened.*

I saw a Best Buy ad in which Best Buy employees were talking directly to the camera: "We heard the feedback that we were hard to find and often didn't seem to know what we were talking about. Now you'll find a knowledgeable blue shirt always available in every department."

You spoke, we listened.

Three different clients in different industries. One smart strategy. That's the type of value an agency can bring to you that's hard to create on your own if you're only focused on your own business or industry.

Many big brands build internal agencies, and this makes sense in a lot of ways. But the problem with it is the myopic focus on just one brand. An internal agency will never have the holistic vision of the market, industry, or cultural landscape.

Agencies are also great cultural curators. My former boss used to say that great ads are an intersection of a product truth, a consumer need, and a cultural moment.

Almost nobody thinks of the cultural moment, but that's always the thing that makes an ad great or makes a video go viral. Here are some examples.

- Oreo: "Dunk in the Dark"

- Volkswagen: "The Force"

- Dove: "Real Beauty"

- Always: "#LikeAGirl"
- Budweiser: "Wassup"
- Nike: "Just Do It"

All of these viral ads and campaigns exploded because of how well the brand aligned with a popular cultural moment or sentiment. Every commercial people love has more to do with the cultural intersection than the product. Genius-level work is when the product truth intersects perfectly with the cultural moment.

Brands keep trying to re-create the dunk-in-the-dark viral moment, but you can't catch lightning in a bottle. You *can* stay on top of cultural trends and be ready to react when things happen, and that's what agencies do. You can't do that by yourself or with your marketing team.

A production company by itself doesn't have those chops.

That is why you want a hybrid shop and internal strategy and creative resources.

That is why it is absolutely crucial that you find a hybrid shop with the sophistication of an agency. You don't want to pull your work from the agency and then start having your team play the agency role.

A creative production company needs to have brand expertise, and it must know how to build and use brand systems and libraries if it is to take the place of your agency. They need to have the pulse on the industry and the market. They need to be astute cultural curators. This is what differentiates a creative production company from a traditional production company. Production companies do not have that type of brand and cultural sophistication because they depend on agencies for that.

In this way a creative production shop can replace many of the most valuable services of an agency while having the added benefit of being able to make creative assets at the drop of a hat to be able to respond to any cultural moment as it's happening.

I mentioned a couple of other items. Clearly, I think it's worth it to concentrate strategy resources with the client. I also think the client should invest in creative resources. An internal agency is not a *bad* idea. It is not a holistic idea. A smarter tactic is to invest in creative resources for your brand.

Inevitably, internal agencies can never handle all the work and they end up contracting out overflow work anyway.

Better to have a creative team that is part of the marketing team and works with all of the vendors. There is no either/or. The internal resources manage the external ones and then everyone is on the same page. The work looks consistent, is equally informed, and there's no politics.

It's surprising to me that brand marketing teams don't usually have internal creatives. Some do, but from my experience it is definitely the exception, not the rule. If you're building an organization from scratch, an efficient ad machine would have an internal marketing team, internal strategy, and a small internal creative team.

If I were the client setting up a department like this, I would want my shops to be content factories, constantly churning out new creative for my digital properties. The highest-performing creative would run on TV.

If one brave marketer did this at one big brand, it would completely disrupt the advertising industry. The ROI would be staggering.

Other than the politics, the model would not be that hard to build. It's a lot less complicated than the existing paradigm.

Now, if you're running this organization, how in control are you feeling? Strategy is right there. Creative at its core is being driven from your team. You have a creative production shop cranking out content and tracking the market and the cultural landscape. You have your fingers on the pulse.

When the lights go out at the Super Bowl, who's ready? You.

Before, you were waiting on the agency to deliver a strategy you were pretty sure was going to be a bit off, cycling through campaign concepts, testing janky animatics, cycling through ad concepts, testing them, shooting them, running them, and then "optimizing" down to one or two spots before starting the process all over again.

Now you're constantly putting new creative into market. The process costs less and takes much less time. All the testing is in-market. You iterate super quickly. You're sure what's going to perform well on broadcast because it was the top performer in your digital channels. Life is good. You get a bonus.

One of the biggest benefits of this model is that instead of internal resources taking a backseat to overpriced agency versions of themselves, they can now take center stage with increased budget and resources. Now you have people that can work directly with a production company, create all your presentation materials, and quickly put concepts together. In your building.

This allows these resources to flourish, which is a massive benefit to the company overall. And as the brand marketing executive, you now have a massive new tool at your disposal available for your direct use, versus through an expensive game of telephone.

This setup can have massive benefits to a brand marketing function and will result in massive ROI for a brand.

How to Find the Right Creative Production Company

Okay, so you're sold. You read the last chapter and you were thinking, *I want that*. Now you have to find the right shop. Many shops talk a big game, but not all can deliver. They're marketers, too. Winky-face. So how do you know what to look for?

Clearly, you're looking for a shop that offers creative/agency services on top of production. Production companies with an agency layer will be more efficient than agencies with production capabilities.

The reason this is the case is . . . agencies have layers and layers of management, while production companies tend to be flatter orgs. Simple as that. Bureaucracy is a killer of creativity and efficiency. Production companies can be more successful adding creative services simply because production companies tend to be flatter organizations with less bureaucracy.

A typical agency account team might look like this:

- SVP/director
- VP/account director
- Account director
- Account supervisor
- Account executive
- Associate account executive

That's six layers of management. Yes, not all agencies have all of those roles, but many do. Some have more. Both the strategy and metrics and project management departments probably have the same number of layers. And there could easily be nine hierarchical layers in creative, with a functional split between design and copy:

- SVP/ECD
- VP/ECD
- Executive creative director
- Creative director
- Associate creative director

- Senior designers and senior copywriters
- Designers and copywriters
- Junior designers and junior copywriters
- Illustrators

I mean, I believe in overindexing on creative resources, but not like that. A vertical stack of managers and delegators isn't helping anyone be more creative. A production company doesn't have that many layers of management, and most of the staff they use for jobs is contingent, so it's much easier to adapt a production company to a hybrid shop. Agencies will always be mired in bureaucracy because of all the layers.

The best option is to find a hybrid shop that was built that way from scratch. Irrespective of how they came into existence, what you're looking for is this:

- A track record of success serving clients of your size and stature
  - This is the most important. If you're a big brand you want to know that a small shop can handle the workload.
- Lots of experience versioning, localizing, exporting, and delivering
  - This is often underestimated, because any one video will probably need at least twenty versions.

- Ability to scale up *and* scale down

  - Many shops say they can scale fast. Ask them how they've done it in the past. Ask them what happens when a client leaves. It's important that the shop won't live and die by your account.

- Great creative

  - Duh.

- Great communication

  - Many production shops fail here.

- Brand sophistication

  - This is what distinguishes a creative production company from a production shop.

- Flat organizational structure

  - Bureaucracy . . . booooo!

- Bias for making stuff

  - LFG! That should be their attitude.

Every shop might not have all of this, but you shouldn't hire any shop that doesn't check most of these boxes.

Chapter 11
Hack Your Shop

I f you're reading this section, you own or you're probably an executive at an agency or a production company.

Agency owners, you're still getting campaign work, but you've noticed there's less of it. There's a lot of activity on content creation, and that work isn't coming to you. It's going straight to production shops and *creators*. You've seen other agencies add production capabilities with mixed success. You *know* you need to start producing the creative you concept, but you're not sure how to do it.

Production company owners, you're getting less work from agencies, which was once your never-ending pipeline. You are also seeing a ton of *content creators* that have a fraction of your talent, resources, and knowledge but score work from big brands. You know you need to add agency-creative services to your offering, but you also know this comes with a big risk.

Agency resources are not cheap, and there is a big risk that they don't actually generate any new revenue for you.

Both agencies and production companies need to tread carefully here. The biggest risk on both sides is from culture and organizational memory. It's not enough for agencies to add production capabilities and vice versa, *if* the organization doesn't coalesce into a single creative-production company. If your organization keeps the agency team siloed from the production company, then you just built a mini-version of the dysfunctional, traditional ad-production model. You need creatives that participate in production and production people that are helping to concept the creative. If you end up throwing the work over the wall to the other org, you're doing it wrong.

This is why it's easier to build a creative production company from scratch than to bolt on capabilities. But if you already have a shop, you don't have that luxury, so here's how you re-create your shop.

Transform Your Agency into a Creative Production Company

You've heard the hype: Agencies are old news! I want to jump on board the Creative Production Express! How do I transform my agency into a creative production company?

Agencies everywhere are adding production capabilities. I didn't invent this idea. It only makes sense that they would expand their capabilities vertically while addressing a common complaint.

I've already pointed out that I'm not the first to call out the inefficiencies of the traditional ad agency/production house model. Because of that, there are a whole host of new-school agencies that are rejecting the traditional structure and are focused on only the most value-added services that agencies provide. It is possible to create an agency that is not mired in bureaucracy and does skip all the unnecessary bullshit.

There are also a lot of large and midsize agencies that are simply adding on production capabilities. What makes it extremely difficult for established agencies of this size to add production service is that all the hierarchy and bloat already exists. So while adding production adds a vertical capability, it doesn't necessarily solve the inefficiency issue. Trimming staff will be necessary, too, but it's extremely hard to downsize into efficiency. Organizational memory lasts a long time.

It's far easier to transform a young or small shop, because you don't have all the layers built in. If your shop already has AAEs, it's going to be a hard slog. Do you know what client wants an AAE on their account? Me neither. I know a lot of agency owners and managers think they need to train people up this way, but it's not true.

Anyway, all this layering just distributes the same amount of work between more people and gives some people fake power because now they have a "team." You may be familiar with the macroeconomic axiom Parkinson's Law—"Work expands so as to fill the time available for its completion." You can observe it in action on large account teams. At a certain point, adding bodies to management, strategy, and administrative teams does not result in any more work getting done. The work just ends up getting divided between more people.

Large agencies will need to do some reorgs (code for layoffs). You don't need that many account people. You just don't. Sorry, account people, you're my boys! (And girls! I mean women!)

The whole team needs to be much leaner. Same with the creative team. You know what client is excited when one of the junior creative teams presents to them? Again, me neither. It was always a massive eye roll for me when I was the client. Inside, the client is thinking, why am I paying for on-the-job training? This is not helping me get my job done quicker or better. It's helping the agency. It's not helping me or my brand.

Our big, expensive agency used to begin their brainstorms by writing a PR statement about the campaign and work backward from there.

I am not kidding.

If your agency is nearly that self-focused, cut that shit out right now. Every briefing should begin with the questions, "How can I help my client move the ball down the field? How can I make them look like a hero with the limited budget and timeline they've been given to complete this job?"

Ideally, you want to add production capabilities without

adding to your overall payroll. Your goal is to expand your business and increase your vertical capabilities and realize all the other benefits I discussed—without adding any employees.

You don't need that many people to begin with.
Here's the skeletal staff you'll need when starting out:

- Producer

- Writer

- Director

- Editor/Camera

- VFX artist

Writer/director could be the same person. It's not hard to find editors that can also shoot. Most of them do, and then they can usually do light rigging and electrical as well. Light rigging and electrical are what a key grip and gaffer would be responsible for on bigger jobs.

With five to seven people you can add a production department. We started with six of us. Here's the key: Everyone has to be *awesome*. Not good. Not great. *Awesome*. They have to have all the qualities I listed earlier in the book.

Also key is your producer, who is going to be the key to your ability to scale on a dime or not. Your producer should have the best "Rolodex" in the city. This is how Wild Gravity went from six to sixty when we got our first Amazon job.

Clearly, if you're adding five to seven without adding head count, you've got to lose five to seven. For a large shop this isn't really a big deal, but for a midsize shop it's going to be pretty painful.

For a small shop, this is an existential decision. Hopefully, you're in a position where you can just add the head count as bloat, and bureaucracy shouldn't be an issue for you yet.

The idea is that you want to add a small production team that can make projects themselves *and* has the capability to run other production teams as more and larger jobs come in. This team needs to be able to expand from five to one hundred and then scale back down again.

That's the part many owners don't plan for. You have to plan for growth *and contraction* and growth again because production activity goes in cycles, and macroeconomic activity tends to dictate the relative heat of the market.

Transform Your Production House into a Creative Production Company

If you have a production company . . . boy, are you sick of working with agencies. Just kidding. Don't tell them I said that.

But really, most production shops would be psyched to go direct to brand, so how do you make that happen? What capabilities do you need to add? At minimum, here are the positions you'll need to add to your staff:

- Account supervisor

- Business development

- Creative director

- Copywriter

- Art director

- Media planner

As you add accounts, you're going to need to build teams under these people. The hard part is that talented agency people tend to be FTEs. Of course there's a huge freelance community, but in agency-world it's not as expected to staff up and down by the job as it is in production-world. Still, it is possible to hire freelance first and then convert those you like to full-time positions when the need arises.

The good news is that it's easier to transform a production company into a hybrid shop than the opposite. As stated earlier, production companies are traditionally flatter organizations that already rely on contractors to scale up and down.

Adding creative services to that mix will not be difficult either. Production shops are pretty creative already, but adding designers, writers, and creative directors is easily manageable.

Make sure to hire leadership with Fortune 100 brand experience. You will need a team that speaks that language and has those connections. If you can't land the right meetings, you're not going to get the business. If you can't navigate the corporations and execute on-brand, flawlessly, every time, they're going to go back to their own Big-Huge agency.

Critical to success here is business development. If agencies have been your business pipeline, now you're competing with them and your company will need to build a whole new muscle.

Agencies are laser focused on biz dev, but production companies are often accustomed to business coming to them. A production company transforming to a hybrid shop will need to flip that mentality and get active in business development at every level.

The great thing here is that once you have your first client, you're in business. Start building case studies from there and get them into all of your social channels to build a self-perpetuating funnel.

Build Your Own Creative Production Company

Let's say you're ready to go full space cowboy and build your own creative production company from scratch. This is how you do it.

First, go get twenty years of experience. Kidding/not kidding. I have not been shy about saying that the secret to our success is our experience. We always say we're happy to give away the secret.

The secret is that it took twenty years of building an impeccable career in advertising and marketing. The secret is that I started in sales. The secret is that I got my MBA at night. The secret is that I got a job at an ad agency. The secret is that I went client-side. The secret is that I ran advertising for some really big brands. The secret is that I went service-side again. The secret is that I always delivered. The secret is that when I was ready, I had an incredible network. The secret is that when I was ready, I could land the meetings. The secret is that when I was ready, I could gather the resources to deliver on the project. The secret is that I was always a grinder. The secret is that since my industry experience was so deep, I could see what was broken and I had the know-how to fix it.

The best thing you can do if you want to go down this road is to get a job in the ad industry.

One of the worst things you can do is launch a business with no experience.

It might be a boring message, but it should be an encouraging message if you already have a job in the industry.

Making your own creative production company will take a lot of work and grit. The most important thing is to get experience. A lot of experience. Client-side and agency-side experience.

Your vision has to be crystal clear. So clear that you could post about it on Facebook and ten people would come and work on the idea with you for free because they wanted to help build it. That vision is only able to develop through extensive experience working in the industry, by seeing what works and what doesn't work.

You need to build a network of resources so when the time comes you can get the work done. You need a network to be able to land the meetings. That takes a long time to build up from scratch. It takes decades of establishing yourself as someone who always delivers.

The most important thing you'll need to launch a successful business is at least one client. You should have a good idea of who your first customer will be *before you launch*. Not who your target market is. Obviously you should know that, but you need to know who, specifically, is going to give you money in exchange for the goods or service you provide. If you know who this person or entity is, you're ready to launch. If you don't know who they are, your first priority is to find them. If you can't find that first customer, you don't have a business, you just have an idea—that needs work.

For two decades I worked with and for corporations, always dreaming of starting my own company. How did I know when the time was right to start my own venture? When I became confident I could land Microsoft and Amazon as our first clients, I knew it was time.

Let's say you have the experience, the vision, and the network and you're ready to go. Practically, here is the minimum staff you'll need:

- President: You! The face of the company, a thought-leader, in charge of *the business*. Responsible for all business operations, business development, marketing, hiring/firing, and financial oversight.

- Executive creative director: The one that makes it all happen, implementer, in charge of all things creative. Responsible for all creative and production output, management of creative and production staff, business development. Participates in marketing, hiring/firing, and financial oversight.

- Senior producer: The one that *actually* makes it all happen. Responsible for staffing all productions, all project budgets, and all scheduling. Manages all creative and production staff. Participates in marketing, hiring/ firing, and financial oversight.

- Senior office manager/bookkeeper: Runs the ship, keeps everyone on course. Responsible for all business administration, accounting, forecasting, planning, office supplies, and so on.

- Senior editor/technician/camera: Keeps the machine and all the machines running. Responsible for capture and editing of all content. Manages all editorial, technical, and production staff. Does all the smaller jobs.

- Senior visual effects artist: Makes the magic happen. Responsible for all digital and graphic artistry. Manages all extended VFX staff.

Here's the staff you can add as needed. We tend to hire freelancers for these positions first, and if they're great and the business need is there, we'll hire them as FTEs if they're interested.

- Producers: Run individual jobs. Responsible for budgeting, staffing, and management of projects.
- Editors: Responsible for editing and output of individual projects.
- Visual effects artists: Responsible for digital and graphic artistry for individual projects.

Many founders will be tempted to have a *virtual company*. We believe strongly that one of the keys to our success is our brick-and-mortar studio. While all these different work-style trends have happened, we have always believed in the importance of having a physical location for our business and having the whole team work in the same space. We did some soul-searching on this during the pandemic, but it became clear early on that having a place where we can all work together is crucial to our success.

To build your own hybrid creative production studio, find a space that will fill the following requirements:

- Producer workspace
- Creative workspace
- Office workspace

- Studio space

- Client-facing edit/VFX suites

- Conference room

- Client-friendly amenities

Of course, you only need the physical space if you're going to be able to fill it up, but make sure it's a space where people want to be. Definitely do not get the space until you have your first client.

Before you launch, you're going to need an extensive network of freelancers and contractors. You personally will need to have agency management chops, production management chops, and client management chops. You need to understand finance, accounting, marketing, HR, and even some business law. At the end of the day, whatever someone else at your company doesn't do, you have to do.

How did I know when it was the right time to start a business? I got my MBA in entrepreneurship in 2000. We started Wild Gravity in 2017. Seventeen years is a long time for it not to be the right time yet. There was a good period of time when I thought that my time to start my own thing had passed. What changed?

What changed is I became confident I could get a client. When I was CMO for the content marketing startup, I landed Microsoft as a client for them. I got them vendor status, and all of the initial Microsoft jobs. If you're a vendor of any kind, you know that just getting vendor status at a big corporation is a big deal. I thought, *I just developed a pretty big piece of business. I bet I could do that again for me.*

When I realized I could do that, I knew I was ready.

I want to reemphasize, if you're considering starting a shop, the most important thing you need is a client. I might have said that, but you'd be amazed at the number of people who pitch businesses that consider that requirement last. They've got their five-year plan, worked out their "exit strategy," and yet they have no idea who their first customer is going to be.

People pitch a lot of business ideas to me and Jonathan. Our first questions are always, how does it make money? Who are your customers going to be? You'd be amazed at how many of these would-be entrepreneurs can't answer those two questions.

We started with that question. We are entirely bootstrapped, so we've had to be profitable since day one. It helps to have that focus. We both hear, all the time, "It must be so satisfying to own your own business." We always say, "It alternates between incredibly satisfying and existentially terrifying."

Don't underestimate the existentially terrifying part. You must have a plan to ride out those parts and have the stomach for it. Overconfidence here is a killer. Macroeconomic factors beyond your control can potentially destroy your business. Per Mike Tyson, "Everyone has a plan until they get punched in the mouth."[6] We had a great plan until about March 2020. There are some things you can't plan for.

When you're first starting a business, don't waste time working on your five-year plan. Get a customer. Get another customer. Revenue is your friend. Everything else flows from there.

If there's one takeaway from all this, it's that there's a lot of bullshit in this industry. Skip all that BS and go to market!

---

6   Mike Tyson, "Everyone Has a Plan 'Till They Get Punched in the Mouth," YouTube, MMA Source, 6:05, https://www.youtube.com/watch?v=qSuMgOu8QPo.

Everyone Asks, "Why Wild Gravity?"

've been a massive Talking Heads fan ever since I saw the original release of *Stop Making Sense* at the Coolidge Corner Theatre in Brookline, Massachusetts, in 1984. Many of their songs are among my favorites, and "Naive Melody" is probably the most perfect, beautiful song in the world. In fact, if the song title sounded cool, "Naive Melody" would be the name of our company. "I Get Wild/Wild Gravity" is also an incredible, beautiful song from Talking Heads' *Speaking in Tongues* album. For a long time I thought "Wild Gravity" would be a cool name for something and I had it filed away in a corner of my brain.

When I thought of the ad agency consultancy idea, I started registering Wild Gravity URLs as a placeholder name. When we considered it, we thought it was a great metaphor for us because gravity is a force that you can either harness or resist. I'm a skier, so I love using gravity to my benefit.

Our logo represents a gravity assist. Wikipedia defines a gravity assist as "a maneuver, swing-by, or generally a gravitational slingshot in orbital mechanics . . . a type of spaceflight flyby which makes use of the relative movement (e.g. orbit around the sun) and gravity of a planet or other astronomical object to alter the path and speed of a spacecraft, typically to save propellant and reduce expense."[7]

This is a perfect metaphor for Wild Gravity. We help our clients to harness existing forces to increase velocity, save propellant, and reduce expense.

Small Fish, Big Sea, Large Appetite

We are now in our eighth year. Microsoft and Amazon are our biggest clients and have been our core clients all eight years. We've also created work for T-Mobile, LEGO, Coca-Cola, the Seahawks, the NBA, Zeiss, KEXP, Alaska Airlines, Pearl Jam, Nintendo, Brooks Running, DomainTools, and many others.

---

7 Wikipedia, "Gravity assist," last updated October 6, 2024, https://en.wikipedia.org/wiki/Gravity_assist.

We feel lucky and proud to have worked with such a marquee list of brands.

We're still a small player in a huge industry, but our model *is working* and people are noticing. We are not the only ones in on this reshaping of the ad production landscape. There are many new-school hybrid creative production shops with different ways of attacking the issue. We don't believe anyone can make higher-quality creative more efficiently than we can. Because of all the reasons I spelled out in the book, our team can produce the highest-quality video assets in the quickest possible timeline, delivered flawlessly.

We are not cheap. There are lots of cheap options. We are not that.

For those working with large agencies and production companies, we represent a massive savings. For those that seek high-production-value video content, we are a fraction of the cost of the traditional ad production route.

The plan for the immediate future is to grow Wild Gravity as big as we can in the Pacific Northwest and then to make more of them. We think brick and mortar is key to what we do. We can and do shoot anywhere and everywhere in the world, and our goal is to have production hubs in the major regions of the United States. Our plan is to find underperforming production studios in the regions we'd like to enter, buy them out over time, and transform them to our model and methodologies.

We imagine a network of four to six Wild Gravities across the country could service the whole United States. We haven't planned beyond that, but there's no reason this model couldn't be copied and expanded globally.

For the near future, our Seattle location could easily handle four to five times the volume, and we're relentlessly focused on that. Anyone interested in producing the best advertising creative of their careers *and* interested in creating a system to make it a repeatable process should reach out to us through our website.

www.wildgravity.net

Anyone seeking courses, e-books, or additional materials from Jon Sneider should visit the author's website. Special offers are available for all readers of *Hacking Advertising*.

www.hackingadvertising.com/offer

Acknowledgments

This book would not have happened without the incredible people I worked with and for throughout my career. Thanks to all the inspiring leaders and amazing colleagues and friends from Digitas, Mullen, Fidelity Investments, L.L.Bean, Microsoft, Redfin, and Contend. Thank you to all the past and present employees, partners, and clients at Wild Gravity. Special thanks to my business partner Jonathan Harris. I literally couldn't have done it without you.

For the book itself, thank you to Joshua Sprague, who taught me how to write a book. Chris Wooster for the first monster edit. To all the early readers and reviewers and to all the project managers, editors, and designers that brought the book to life and to market. And most of all thank you to my family. Ellen, Max, and Sadie, it's all worth it because of you.

About the Author

Raised in Boston during the '70s and '80s, Jon Sneider moved west to study at Colorado College, graduating with a degree in comparative literature in 1991. After a few years serving drinks and skiing in Telluride, he returned to Boston to begin a career in marketing, cutting his teeth selling Wave Radios for Bose over the phone. His knack for sales saw him manage a $20-million sales team while earning his MBA at night.

After earning his degree, he joined Digitas, Inc., one of the earliest and largest interactive agencies in the US. By the new millennium, he was responsible for supervising digital accounts for industry giants like GM, AT&T, Microsoft, and Time-Warner. This position served as an excellent springboard for his subsequent twenty-five-year career in advertising and marketing.

He moved from agency to client-side when he transitioned to Fidelity Investments to lead the revamp of fidelity.com.

Subsequently, he was recruited by L.L. Bean as director of advertising & brand, expanding his skill set to broadcast advertising, producing national television and digital advertising campaigns.

When a former boss from Fidelity moved to Microsoft, offering Sneider a role managing advertising for Windows, he moved his family west, to Seattle. There he worked with the nation's largest and most coveted ad agencies executing on eight-figure budgets. After five years at Microsoft, he joined Redfin as VP of advertising and brand, managing their first-ever broadcast advertising campaign. While working with these influential brands, he recognized inefficiencies in advertising production.

Realizing that globally recognized creative content could be produced more efficiently without relying on ad agencies, he was inspired to launch Wild Gravity in 2017. In just three months, with no initial capital, employees, or physical infrastructure, the company secured two trillion-dollar corporations as its first clients and became a multimillion-dollar company in its first year.

Wild Gravity's unique process allows the team to deliver work superior to traditional agencies' to some of the world's biggest brands more quickly and cost-effectively. The success of this approach inspired him to author *Hacking Advertising.*